AF444226

Collaborators:

Laura Battistella, freelance translator and interpreter
Clive Best, Physicist
Emilio Guariglia, journalist, text redactor
Vittorio Introcaso, RAI2 journalist
Davide Peluzzi, President of Explora Nunaat International, explorer

Pictures by Davide Peluzzi excepting:
Antartic, lawn of ice by Mauro Dolci, Fig. 10.8
Himalaya at sunset by Nino Carlini, Fig. 10.9
Gran Sasso, spring 2013 by Biagio Mengoli, Fig. 10.15

Prefaces by:
Prof. Augusta Busico, General Secretary UGEF
European Journalist Union for Federalism
President of Scientific Association "Età verde", www.verdegreen.net

Pinuccio D'Aquila, geologist, glaciologist

Roberto Madrigali

The Future of the Earth is written on the Moon

How to know and analyze climate change
predict the weather that will came
and get ready for a new Ice Age

Youcanprint *Self-Publishing*

Youcanprint Self-Publishing
Via Roma, 73 - 73039 Tricase (LE) - Italy
www.youcanprint.it
info@youcanprint.it
Facebook: facebook.com/youcanprint.it
Twitter: twitter.com/youcanprintit

ISBN 978-88-91169-55-6

I edition: November 2013

Contents

Preface

I tell you about the climate change

It is like a narration, a fascinating, wonderful, terrifying and reassuring story: let's flick together through the Great Book of the Time and read Roberto Madrigali's pages about climate changes. Under our eyes is the story of the planet Earth between alternating cold and hot periods with the inevitable changes, the migrations of entire populations, the drama of generations: we cannot change the past but we can learn for the future how history, intended in the best way, should teach us.

And here is the new Aeolus, lord of winds and currents, the Jet Stream of the free atmosphere playing a decisive role in the climate changes. The American pilots flying up and down the Hawaii during the second world war, the Top Guns, discovered it: by flying high they used to come across strong turbulences, despite the weather forecast said the contrary. Another two evocative places go down in the history of climate: the Poles and vortexes Arctic and Antarctic. Two essential elements which play an important role for the penetration of the cold air southwards, moved by nature to balance the big thermal difference existing between the polar and equatorial–tropical latitudes.

However, as in all respectable stories, also here we meet the "Lady" on whom the Jet Stream depends, the Moon, the star which has always nourished human fantasies. The Moon, with its gravitational force, is the keystone of all the process, gives input to the Jet Stream configuration movements and therefore to the planet climatic evolutions and can allow accurate long–term weather forecast. The tides, which depend on the Moon, are another fascinating element: but why does the Moon influence the tides (and tropospheric flow) and why not the Sun which is also an infinitely bigger body? All these questions are answered by the "Tesi Madrigali — Meteo Mundi" here illustrated and documented from the narration which seems fantastic to the scientific rigor: a publication for everybody, an educational aid which teachers can use for teaching to young people and in the permanent education, useful to public and private bodies, to farmers' associations, to tourism. Today, as the European Union said recently, it is easy to realise how the information in terms of climate changes is missing or hardly mentioned.

These references are at the basis of the collaboration established for years between the Group on Macroproblems "Aurelio Peccei" of the Green Age Association and the Association Explora, presided over by Mr. Davide Peluzzi, who intends to contribute to a better understanding of the climate on the Earth through his expeditions in extreme environments such as the Himalaya or the Arctic, in harmony with the studies of the expert Roberto Madragali.

In particular since last year the common interest has been based on the opportunity to make the "mystery" of the terrestrial climatic evolutions decipherable, by following a line of objective research and of communication and dissemination of results.

For this reason the next contests of the Green Age Association, aimed at young people at international level, will have the climate changes and observations on their territory as their basis. Since these evolutions depend on both natural and anthropical cycles, which have great importance and difference from place to place, it is necessary to work at local level on the microclimate where climate changes often have amplified effects.

Therefore the Associations The Green Age and Explora have expressed the need to make experimental models which reproduce actions in limited areas of the Mediterranean area and emblematic of existing and future situations, following monitoring actions of the anthropised impact on the selected areas: in fact, for such an important phenomenon for the future of men and their life standard as well as for the economic development such as the climate change, it is necessary to compare and integrate the data of the Countries interacting in the Mediterranean region, each with its specific characteristics. Hence the elaboration of the project "Young People Meet Climate Change" (Acronym: YOU.MEET), which intends to involve young people by taking the opportunities given by the European Union, in a first stage through a European action of Youth Exchange and later through the participation in the Programme LIFE in 2014.

Every European exchange is a great opportunity of cultural, social and linguistic learning certified thanks to the Youthpass.

We intend to analyse and monitor from time to time some European areas of the Mediterranean area by gathering them according to the following characteristics: Urban, Marine, Rural and Mountain and the results will form a log book in Italian and English which will be used for future research by the young people from the European Countries who will be involved from time to time.

The project action should study in depth the conditions of the existing one, raise the awareness not only of students but also of families and elderly so than they can be the spokespersons of this need at the local authorities. In fact, even if the Mediterranean area has a particular climate action, set in a water reservoir protected by the Alps and intimately influenced by the contiguity of the hottest continent, Africa, it inevitably succumbs to the global variations of the temperature generated by the jet stream of the free atmosphere.

"Act and adapt" are the keywords of the project YOU.MEET, a slogan launched by the European Commission: act in order to prevent the situation from getting worse and adapt, that is properly facing the events which are not attributable to men's actions.

However, whereas the changes of the physical environment are well documented, the data on the specific adaptation interventions are missing: since we need more data on the adaptation costs, it is important to involve our society, the business world and the European public sector in the preparation of coordinated adaptation strategies: that is action plans on health, vaccinations, health system planning, planning for the risks of floods, management of drought crises and water scarcity, protection of coasts and against floods, economic diversification, strengthening of public and private buildings, management of the use of land and increase in green in cities. It is said that the Mediterranean area will be one of the areas mostly affected in terms of energy demand, agricultural productivity, water availability, impact on health, summer tourism and ecosystem. Hence the need of a reliable information to all citizens and their decision–making bodies to start from 2013 the "European Year of the active citizenship".

Augusta Busico
Teacher and journalist
General Secretery UGEF (European Journalist Union for Federalism)
President of the Scientific Association The Green Age (verdegreen.net)

Preface

The issue of climate change and weather forecast trill millions of people and the net is full of sites or weather enthusiasts.

Therefore, I think this text could be appreciated by many fans and not thanks to the divulgate language that has been adopted in its drafting, as it allows to acquire some basic knowledge to know the great dynamics of the atmosphere.

During my brief research period, I developed an interest in environmental issues and climate change, at the same time I grow fond to meteorology, and during my studies, I had the opportunity to observe abnormalities, especially on the Calderone Glacier (Gran Sasso of Italy) above other alpine glaciers that makes me think focus on Global Warming…

This theory is very compelling because it is also linked to the lunar cycles; it provides evidence of how our natural satellite affects the large atmospheric circulation.

Maybe the key to the weather forecast has always been over our heads and we ever notice it? Or rather, since old ages there were references to the Moon in agriculture and other practices that are related to the the meteorology; perhaps Madrigali has only been able to find out why the Moon affects the weather.

The location of our natural satellite, respect to the Earth and to other celestial bodies, seems to "drive" the big heat exchanges that take place on our planet between the polar regions and equatorial areas, and could influence during its cycles, the climate. On the other hand, we well know theories on climate change based on correlations between climate change and astronomical parameters (see Milankovitch), but in this case they also helps to explain not only the arrival of an ice age, but also the global warming. There are, in fact, references to episodes of "exceptional" cooling and or heating of the atmosphere that are not attributable to the lunar cycles according to the author.

The theory of Madrigali should not cheer up a lot because questioning global warming opens the door to new scenarios that could be just as dangerous, or at least confirm that we do not go to the climatic optimum.

Hoping to have intrigued enough without anticipate too much, I wish you a good reading.

Pinuccio D'Aquila
Geologist and glaciologist

Introduction

The salmon who flew to the Moon. A handbook of preparation for an extraordinary journey

If a salmon one day, by accident or intention, opposed to the strength of ocean currents and abandoned the route marked out from the crowd, certainly, by itself, would increase the chances of ending up as food for predators. At the same time, he would have the opportunity to see that in the sea there is not just one single current, and that not all currents lead the ambush of fishing vessels.

The sudden deviation of the "rebel" salmon and its consequences have a close relationship with the genesis of the greatest scientific discoveries, always result of the ability of one or more men to observe things — whether they are physical phenomena or constructions of thought — from a different angle than the one that appears marked by fate. Sometimes this heterodox look opens for coincidences, as told by the legendary Sir Isaac Newton's apple. More often the case for deliberate choices and tough such as those of Galileo or Copernicus eyes of which traveled in the elsewhere of the Universe (without satellites or spaceships!) to refute the irrefutable dogma of Ptolemy.

This publication, which is a candidate to redesign what we have just given for acquired as part of meteorology, wants to bring to the attention of the international scientific community — and disseminate between the merely curious or lovers of the sector — The Theory of Madrigali — Meteo Mundi Project. This Theory is an organic assumption about the origins of terrestrial climate change that is the result of research carried out for years by Roberto Madrigali, supported by a weighty amount of technical data and, finally, supported or looked upon with great interest by undisputed authorities.

The Theory of Madrigali — Meteo Mundi — grew out of currents and turns. Madrigali could follow another current — "physical" — breaking with the main school of thought and with it he reached amazing destinations formulating a theory that, with the simplicity of numbers and empirical evidences, returns to humanity a very different destiny than the one that today is attributed for granted.

This predominant school of thought is known under the name of Global Warming. Noting that in some regions of the world the climate did not follow the period of cyclical stability ("Seasons are not what they use to be!"[1] The catchphrase of the last thirty years) and an overall rising of temperatures, at the end of the last century scientists began to hypothesize an irreversible process of warming of the Earth, with all the disastrous consequences of the case. The consequences are advancement of desert areas, melting of glaciers, rising levels of seas and oceans, in addition to the concatenation of a series of unusual phenomena, such as a succession of long drought and strong, and unexpected precipitations.

This theory contradicted what the science had taken for granted since the pioneering researches of the early nineteenth century. Earth's destiny was the cooling down for the arrival — sooner or later — of one of cyclical ice ages, more or less important, that have marked the last million years of history at almost regular intervals. The most recent one calls "Little Ice Age" between 1400/1500 and 1870. Therefore, the climate optimum in which the humanity was living during the latest 2/3 centuries was a privileged pause between a great cold and the other. Who is more than forty years old, will remember the inevitable picture of the dying and ice–bound mammoths in his first school's book. Planetary Hibernation, as much as the inevitable shutdown of the Sun, is an image imprinted in the mind and a perspective, which disturb sleep.

Today, however, we are all certain that the threat of extinction for the human race (and not only) will arrive from the heat. The average temperature will grow at an exponential and irreversible rate, and soon the Earth will be a blast furnace from which no one will escape. In the collective imagination, sad eyes of the frozen mammoth replaced by the wonders of computer graphics used in movies, documentaries and television. Icebergs liquefying like butter in saucepan, tsunamis

---

1. Translator note: typical Italian expression that is usually used to emphasize the constant change of the climate, then the lack of well–defined seasons and with features outlined before alternated with greater constancy.

swallowing up the skyscrapers of New York City and the Basilica of San Marco, pets' carcasses scattered in a Saharan–like house yard.

To determine this sudden overturn of dominant thought (and nightmare), and to make the theory of Global Warming virtually indisputable, contributed in a decisive manner the perfect weld between this hypothesis and the emergence of the modern environmental consciousness.

To explain a new climate phenomenon occurred at the end of the last century: rising temperatures, the melting of glaciers, the advance of deserts, derailment of the seasons from the usual binary, someone considered plausible to relate it with the other big process of those years, the historical peak of industrialization (and hence pollution) global, accelerated from access to the "modernity" of countries such as China and India.

The equation pollution = overheating = disruption of the climate, even before it for its scientific basis, becomes dogma in short time because is extremely functional for the ecologist cause. Who rightly care about the defense of human health and the environment had never found in his hands a weapon so powerful (the threat of the end of the World!) in support of his battles. The need to curb human aggression on Nature and climate sciences have instituted an indissoluble partnership of "mutual assistance", one feeding the other: the desire to save the World invokes investment in research on the Global Warming, the research suggests substantial investments against pollution (see the Kyoto Protocol) to save the world from Global Warming.

No one can deny the fact that this "relationship" had some important and positive effects on environmental protection. In a few years, it has instill even in the lazier minds (usually those of rulers) and refractories to the common good (as those of executives), the awareness that poisoning the Earth and destroying her genetic heritage is also an attack against the future of humanity. At least, it has imposed a global reflection on the obligation to balance the importance of economic wealth with the protection of the welfare of the species; it also has accelerated the use of alternative energy sources and production methods less dangerous for the human health. No one will ever regret these results, although there is a lot to achieve.

The same cannot be said about the "partner". That from this relationship has mainly gained a constraint. Overwhelmed by the echo of environmental cause, the climatological science, even if "young" and needing to grow without prejudice, suddenly stops, enclosing its sight in the horizon of the single thought. The certainty that the man, polluting, is the author of the climate changes has overshadowed all other possibilities. Not only inhibiting any temptation to formulate alternative hypotheses, as it should be instead the practice of good science, but also even forgetting everything that science had revealed so far.

The Earth's history is full of climate "distortions" much more powerful than those recorded in recent decades. Analyzing only the closer past, we can observe that, in a century, from the late nineteenth to the late twentieth everything is happened from the optimum climate of the fifties (in spite of wars and atomic bombs), to thirty years of cold climate that follows and finally the return of the heat from the eighties onwards. A period of time so limited (ridiculous, compared with the age of the planet) is sufficient to tell the strong thermal mutability of the Earth and repetitive rhythmic cadence — which is immutable in which hot cycles and cold cycles will alternate.

If we think of a more distant past, we can understand better how climatic oscillations are "physiological" even when they are brought to the extremes with virulence and persistence. The historical documents and in–depth research on climate change and on the core borings of glaciers offered valuable and accurate information.

For example, the interglacial age in which we live and which is now 11,500 years old is ending. Well, this has already lived a very hot period in its central part, between 5500 and 2400 BC, with high temperatures. In that specific time, the ice melted to such an extent that the sea rose by four meters above the present level. A few thousand years later, between 800 and 1200 AD — in the so–called optimum medieval — sea levels rose of between 50 centimeters and one meter, and icebergs almost disappeared. Then around In 1400, came the colder, longer and more severe period in interglacial memories. the Little Ice Age, in fact, that is increased between 1500 and 1870, alternating cold winters to summers often disturbed, also a surprising (but not frequent) periods with mild winters and dry summers.

In short, there was never a lack of apparent oddities and sudden revolutions of climate. For example, the expression "Seasons are not what they use to be!" was popular between old people at the dawn Renaissance.

Although so many prior events constitute a strong clue (a clue should never be ignored), they shall not constitute sufficient evidence to demonstrate that the current climate of the planet is the result of one of those ordinary fluctuations so clearly attested in diachrony. We can hypothesize that massive doses of CO_2 and poisons in the atmosphere can change the physiological order and emphasize the extreme tendencies causing an unpredictable overheating with catastrophic consequences. Unpredictable? Responding to this question, we could find the "solid proof" that the Global Warming theory causing by greenhouse effect is not the right scientific explanation to the last climate events.

In fact, if there was something, a sort of "constant" on the basis of which we can show how this unusual (in living memory) hot cycle was actually always predictable: that means that it should happened now by natural necessity and not by human will and that accidentally it coincides with the historical peak of pollutant emissions; well, we would have two strong indications. As detective stories funs knows, we just need one more to have an evidence.

In the Madrigali Theory we can find that "something" that was missed. It is a current returning to the journey of our salmon. A current in the literal sense that does not dominate scientific thought, but manages to stick climatic changes on Earth.

We are talking about the wind or Jet Stream; the jet stream of free flowing tireless atmosphere above our heads since the birth of the planet, at a variable speed of all respect (ranging between 80 and 200 kilometers per hour) and bound to the observation of the polar vortex, depression in this cold character in a permanent and increasingly in share on Arctic areas.

Although known for some time now, the Jet Stream — comparable to the wind breeze that blows over the sea, but instead flows into the upper atmosphere between 5 and 15 kilometers from the ground — has never been taken too much into account by those who study the mutations climate on Earth and their origins. Indeed in recent decades has been all but ignored by most of the scientific community. All thoughtful look at man's height, all aiming at evaluating the effects of what goes from the bottom to the top (the smoke from the chimneys), meteorologists and climatologists have abandoned the old, and in this field healthy habit, of looking up to the sky. The Madrigali theory reverses this perspective.

Intrigued by the Jet Stream, Roberto Madrigali for years has studied "moves", put them in relation with the "movements" of other natural forces (the Sun, the polar vortex, the Great general circulation of the atmosphere) and finally, after he applied them with the most scientific rigor, empirical evidence of climate variability of the Earth. Not only the diachronic variability, fluctuations in time, but also to the synchronic one: think for example — at the same time and on the same parallel — to the huge difference between "air" in New York and Naples, or between a walk in Tuscany and one in Northern Japan.

The conclusions are clear and striking: the jet stream, or Jet Stream, is the "dominus" of the choices climate of the planet, is the main triggering element of the changes that have always characterized the Earth.

There is an atmospheric process determined by the presence of the Sun, the star closest to us. The Sun is the driving force energy (fuel) of the entire system, and the Jet Stream is the means by which the Great general circulation of the atmosphere distributes this energy, in time and in space, under the direction — expansive or — contraction of the polar vortex.

In this complex as perfect mechanism the jet stream high altitude has therefore a strategic role, a specific task assigned to transport the different masses of air temperature at different latitudes, thus giving substantial changes of weather and climate occurring at rates well marked, also repetitive and extreme.

The Jet Stream, in short, has always commanded the bluntly climatic conditions throughout the entire world. If anyone could interfered with its temporal evolution, which proceeds in regular cycles of two to four weeks, he would have an unimaginable power: the power to determine precise changing climate on specific areas of the planet, such as by imposing a powerful and persistence destructive ice, drought or torrential rains. If Hitler had had the control of the Jet Stream, might have melted the snow, which prevented his troops to conquer Stalingrad, Napoleon stop the storm and win at Waterloo and Osama Bin Laden engulf the White House under ten years of hurricanes.

The jet stream, however, does not take orders from man. For better or for worse. Unperturbed, for millions of years, performs its task with precision worthy of an employee Switzerland. A constant, as will demonstrate further the scientific data that underpin the Theory of Madrigali, that not even the pollution from CO_2 can touch.

The Jet Stream is the vehicle of the Earth's climate, the idea that a man's choice, the poisoning of the air, can somehow change the trajectories of space and time is roughly equivalent to the conclusion that the ritual of the shaman Indians can really make the rain fall.

The Theory of Madrigali, therefore, rejects the direct connection between anthropogenic pollution and the contingent current warming of the Earth. In doing so denies the prospect of Global Warming, with all its catastrophic consequences, if anything, opening the door to the expectation of Global Cooling, the cyclical return of glaciation.

Is this a reassuring theory? Not really, actually anything but that.

First, and it is worth pointing out, no one think to be able to translate this scientific theory in a eulogy of the polluting practices. Spreading poisons in the air we breathe, poisoning the seas, to slaughter the biodiversity, clearing the forests, is a crime, because it erases the welfare of all living species and often results in actual murder, be it small–scale or large scale. The Theory of Madrigali says simply that there is a direct link between these behaviors and climatic changes taking place. In short, spraying poison gas in the atmosphere will bring humanity to extinction by suffocation or pandemics tumor, but not by drowning in the waters of the glaciers melted.

Furthermore, it is also clear that denying the man the right to determine, in evil as in good, at least the evolution of the climate, and through it the end of the world, comes down to the recognition of the supremacy of Nature and the need to respect it. Paradoxically, to affirm that the human being is able to induce a weather catastrophe, it also means give it the power to do the opposite, in fact to control the forces of nature. Since we all know that is not like that (earthquakes, tsunamis, famines, and ice ages them even those who suffered in the atmosphere emitted little else that his breath), a modest escape anthropocentrism will be beneficial. Even at the cost of having to accept the disturbing prospect that eventually, when nature will strike, we will have very few means to protect ourselves.

In this regard, finally, certainly cannot reassure the announcement based on scientific findings of an imminent return to the ice age. If we are afraid of dying, there will be no differs between cold or heat.

The Madrigali Theory, therefore, cannot reassure us. No one has ever focus on the problem. A scientific theory that had an objective psychological reassurance terrorism that everything could be defined except scientific theory.

On one point, however this theory, in its development linked to the project Meteo Mundi, could offer a service to humanity, concrete and useful. The Jet Stream as mentioned nourished by the Sun, following contractions of the polar vortex and distributes energy on behalf of the Great General Circulation of the Atmosphere. All according to precise intervals. Who does, or what, determine these frequencies?

Once again, a question and an answer, which may throw open the door to the third clue, what it takes to form the evidence. In fact, if it was possible to attribute this cyclical Jet Stream action to its interaction with a determined time cycles force and length we could be able to determine also when the Jet Stream will trigger certain meteorological times of and how much these will last. That means the man would be offered the opportunity to advance forecasts of absolute precision in a very long time, infinitely longer than those of which we are capable today.

The only force that really affects the jet stream high altitude, is the Moon as Roberto Madrigali tells us. Yes, the same Moon that poets have always describe as delicate and romantic, and that instead it is now proposed as a key element for the understanding of global climate inconstancies.

Crossing the regularity of the lunar movements to those of the Sun and the Earth; comparing the result with the movements of the Jet Stream and then superimposing all the climatic changes of the past near and far, Madrigali and his team arrive to a truth able to delight them the same persons who had formulated it. The Moon, in a complex game of vector forces, regulates the timing of climate changes on Earth. Forever and more. Following the lunar orbits is possible to predict, "What the weather will do" and thus the major processes global climate from here to the next decades.

That the Moon could influence "good and bad weather" thought, farmers and fishermen for millennia, carving those feelings in proverbs curiously similar to each other in every age and in every corner of the globe.

As scientists are well aware because of the tides the Moon affects Earth "moods", as poets imagined: *It is the very error of the Moon, she comes more nearer Earth than she was wont and makes men mad.*

Shakespeare writes in the *Othello*, and Chagall draws that power in endless dreams in which the World people, animals, things and cities levitates for lunar energy.

The theory of Madrigali and Meteo Mundi take it a step further. They ignore and fantastic and folkloric suggestions, leave evidence of the tide phenomenon and apply it with scientific rigor to a huge river of air, the Jet Stream. In this way, they demonstrate the decisive role of the Moon in the climatic vicissitudes of the Earth.

A discovery that could give you a big help to humanity, allowing time to gear up for a disaster waiting to happen, not far now, the arrival of a new Ice Age. This should prompt the scientific communities and governments to ask questions and encourage research.

In these pages you will read all this and much more, dense data and "facts" that reconstruct the remarkable journey made by Theory of Madrigali.

At least, you can believe it or not. It will still be worth it. Exit from common places, free from the mainstream, look at the world from a new perspective, cast an eye on a future different from what everyone thinks: from the journey of the salmon to the wonderful climate discover about JS and the Moon; however, has been a wonderful adventure.

Have a good trip.

Some good reasons for not accepting the dogma of Global Warming

"The Sun is God!" cried JMW Turner as he died, and plenty of other people have thought there was much in his analysis. The Aztecs agreed, and so did the pharaohs of Egypt. We are an arrogant lot these days, and we tend to underestimate the importance of our governor and creator.

We forget that we were once just a clod of cooled–down solar dust; we forget that without the Sun there would have been no photosynthesis, no hydrocarbons — and that it was the great celestial orb that effectively called life into being on Earth. In so far as we are able to heat our homes or turn on our computers or drive to work it is thanks to the unlocking of energy from the Sun.

As a species, we human beings have become so blind with conceit and self–love that we genuinely believe that the fate of the planet is in our hands — when the reality is that everything, or almost everything, depends on the behaviour and caprice of the gigantic thermonuclear fireball around which we revolve.

I say all this because I am sitting here staring through the window at the flowerpot and the bashed–up barbecue, and I am starting to think this series of winters is not a coincidence. The snow on the flowerpot, since I have been staring, has got about an inch thicker. The barbecue is all but invisible. By my calculations, this is now the fifth year in a row that we have had an unusual amount of snow; and by unusual I mean snow of a kind that I don't remember from my childhood: snow that comes one day, and then sticks around for a couple of days, followed by more.

I remember snow that used to come and settle for just long enough for a single decent snowball fight before turning to slush; I don't remember winters like this. Two days ago I was cycling through Trafalgar Square and saw icicles on the traffic lights; and though I am sure plenty of readers will say I am just unobservant, I don't think I have seen that before. I am all for theories about climate change, and would not for a moment dispute the wisdom or good intentions of the vast majority of scientists.

But I am also an empiricist; and I observe that something appears to be up with our winter weather, and to call it "warming" is obviously to strain the language. I see from the BBC website that there are scientists who say that "global warming" is indeed the cause of the cold and snowy winters we seem to be having. A team of Americans and Chinese experts have postulated that the melting of the Arctic ice means that the whole North Atlantic is being chilled as the floes start to break off — like a Martini refrigerated by ice cubes.

I do not have the expertise to comment on the Martini theory; I merely observe that there are at least some other reputable scientists who say that it is complete tosh, or at least that there is no evidence to support it. We are expecting the snow and cold to go on for several days, and though London transport has coped very well so far, with few delays or cancellations, I can't help brooding on my own amateur meteorological observations. I wish I knew more about what is going on, and why. It is time to consult once again the learned astrophysicist, Piers Corbyn.

Now Piers has a very good record of forecasting the weather. He has been bang on about these cold winters. Like JMW Turner and the Aztecs he thinks we should be paying more attention to the Sun. According to Piers, global temperature depends not on concentrations of CO_2 but on the mood of our celestial orb. Sometime too bright the eye of heaven shines, said Shakespeare, and often is his gold complexion dimmed. That is more or less right. There are times in astronomical history when the Sun has been churning out more stuff — protons and electrons and what have you — than at other times. When the Sun has plenty of sunspots, he bathes the Earth in abundant rays.

When the solar acne diminishes, it seems that the Earth gets colder. No one contests that when the planet palpably cooled from 1645 to 1715 — the Maunder minimum, which saw the freezing of the Thames — there was a diminution of solar activity. The same point is made about the so–called Dalton minimum, from 1790 to 1830. And it is the view of Piers Corbyn that we are now seeing exactly the same phenomenon today.

Lower solar activity means — broadly speaking — that there is less agitation of the warm currents of air from the tropical to the temperate zones, so that a place like Britain can expect to be colder and damper in summer, and colder and snowier in winter. *There is every indication that we are at the beginning of a mini ice age he says. The general decline in solar activity is lower than Nasa's lowest prediction of five years ago. That could be very bad news for our climate. We are in for a prolonged cold period. Indeed, we could have 30 years of general cooling.*

Now I am not for a second saying that I am convinced Piers is right; and to all those scientists and environmentalists who will go wild with indignation on the publication of this article, I say, relax. I certainly support reducing CO_2 by retrofitting homes and offices — not least since that reduces fuel bills. I want cleaner vehicles.

I am speaking only as a layman who observes that there is plenty of snow in our winters these days, and who wonders whether it might be time for government to start taking seriously the possibility — however remote — that Corbyn is right. If he is, that will have big implications for agriculture, tourism, transport, aviation policy and the economy as a whole. Of course it still seems a bit nuts to talk of the encroachment of a mini ice age.

But it doesn't seem as nuts as it did five years ago. I look at the snowy waste outside, and I have an open mind.[2]

For millions of years the Earth's climate beats the rhythm of nature and of the thermal changes on our Planet. However, the *modus operandi* and consequences of work of this sophisticated machine are still to explore. Our studies are focused precisely on the composition, internal dynamics and the effects of this powerful gear, concluding that climate variations should be and will have cause for it in the future. It follows in particular, and in an ever more convincing, that human activity that it has no effect on climate change. Or rather, the CO_2[3] emissions pollute our air, kill life on the Planet, but do not alter significantly the balance of Earth's climate.

2. Boris JOHNSON, «The Telegraph», 20/01/2013. Boris JOHNSON one of Britain's best known politicians, and now Mayor of London (official letter from the Mayor of London in disagreement with l'IPCC)

3. Carbon dioxide, also known as the dioxide or carbon dioxide is essential for plant life (photosynthesis) and animals and prevents the planet to cool down significantly.

The shortsighted selfishness of humanity, that in this circumstance aspires to the role of demiurge, is unmasked with macroscopic evidence of past climate evolution, measured by coring[4] and supported by screen–printing[5] and reading of historical documents recorded. A weighty and conclusive amount of data, which show the constant presence of climate change on our Planet. Concisely, especially the coring certify that the Earth has always been characterized by alternating, often bloody ages, of warmer and colder periods. Even in times when there was not just industry, but also not even humanity.

Without wishing to resort to the proverbial "history teacher of life" this compelling factual truth should give us something to reflect on. But today, and in the past few decades, scientific community overwhelming majority erases almost uncritically the weight and meaning of a few million years, limits his observation and assumes the equation "anthropogenic pollution = overheating Earth = irreversible climate disruption" like a dogma.

The dogma of the Global Warming[6] would be accelerated by the human action.

The conjecture of Global Warming, that as a theory must certainly be taken in the highest regard, and for this it would be questioning because it does not seem to respond to the reality of things, can be based solely on a very limited horizon, and this has fragile foundations. It takes into account a limited period (the past half–century) and offers a contingent explanation to the apparent "climate indiscipline" of this short period of time. A reasonable explanation, but not exhaustive.

In fact, you can easily see how this phenomenon happen again. It is not an isolated event. Indeed, in the past, repeatedly, the average temperature of the planet has risen sharply, to cause melting of glaciers and elevations of the seas in proportions far more traumatic. This finding is not enough to deny a possible connection between anthropogenic pollution and average warming of the Planet. It is sufficient to draw an impassable limit to the theory of Global Warming, which we cannot explain because between 5,500 and 2,400 BC, the Earth warmed to the point that seas grew to four feet, before falling

---

4. Core drill: carrot taken from a glacier and is a sampling technique of glaciers.
5. Stratigraphy: branch of study in geology and dating of rocks.
6. Global Warming: theory of anthropogenic global warming.

and back to rise (up to one meter) at the beginning of the Middle Ages. What role can have played the anthropogenic pollution in those terrific events?

Global Warming could offer a specific answer to a specific event. Today we stop pollutant emissions and the impending announced disaster. Then, what? If it has already happened when man was not responsible for pollution, will happen again even if man will not pollute more. What will we do in the near future when the Earth will return either to red–hot or freezing state, as it has always done cyclically throughout its history?

This simple question establish the duty to turn the spotlight off scientific curiosity, free from prejudices and psychological influences, at least on the causes and mechanisms at the origin of the great climatic changes which always shooked the Earth.

The study on the historical climate documents, supported by a thorough analysis of the Great general circulation of the atmosphere[7] and the observation of the expansion and contraction of the Arctic and Antarctic depression (Polar Vortex[8]), led us to a conclusion totally opposed to the theory of anthropogenic global warming. This is the heart of Madrigali Theory. We can now say with certainty of data that the Great Climate Machine has constantly worked over time — regardless of human presence — noting a series of thermal well–defined cadences based on inevitable rules, never interrupted from its origins to the present day and intended to occur with the same evolutionary sequence also in the near future. A careful diachronic analysis allows filling in many gaps in the interpretation of temperature changes and points out the importance to compare the present with the changing climate of the past, so humanity will not be unprepared to the next, and discounted, climate change coming.

Before to understand the functions of Earth's climate from a technical and scientific point of view, it is necessary to clear up possible misunderstandings related to hasty "philosophical interpretations" of our theory.

---

7. GGCA, Great General Circulation of the Atmosphere: at high altitude river of air flowing over the entire planet with two distinct flows, polar and subtropical.

8. Polar Vortex: area of low pressure at high altitude that parked in a semi–permanent over the poles.

Pollution is a crime against life. Failure to comply with international protocols for the limitation of pollutant sources and the development of alternative energy sources is an attack on the future of every living being. The future not exists without respect for life, no future without environment protection.

Pursuing the harmony of the human race with the ecosystem is, even before a requirement for survival, an act of intelligence and respect which clearly reveals the high point of the evolution of Homo sapiens. Education on good environmental practices, exercised in daily work, at school, workplaces, churches, and families through the means of mass communication is the key issue. Instead, the attempt to educate humanity to ecological theme using the terrorist weapon (also very profitable in terms of marketing) of catastrophe is fruitless and regressive. Especially if, as in the case of Global Warming, catastrophe is announced as a truth not based on a solid scientific prediction. Humanity has many tools to exercise its free will on the livability of the planet, from the concrete to the CO_2, from chemistry to nuclear power. We have studied the great climatic changes of the Earth and we can say that now there is human artifice able to determine them in any way. Here, we will not only talk about pollution because this is not a helpful theme to understand the operation of the machine Great climate, aim of our study. This does not mean, however, that the scientific conclusions of this research are functional to endorse any form of human aggression to the environment.

This should subtract arguments to those who wished to delegitimize the Theory of Madrigali, without to refute it in its scientific foundations, accusing it of being in favor of polluters.

Many of the scholars who support the theory of global warming, in fact, support the idea that researchers deny the anthropogenic Global Warming because they are insensitive to the environment, or people paid by "powers" that want a theoretical support to continue the savage exploitation of the Planet. This idea, supported by illustrious luminaries that often are the beneficiaries of an enormous media influence, become a collective opinion. Anyone who dares to question the cause–effect relationship between CO_2 emissions and climate upheavals enters in the black list of the enemies of human health, for this reason, what he says is not even taken into consideration. The paradoxical result: in a hyper–technologic hyper–scientific and hyper–laic society of the third millennium, there is a science (not a faith!), the Climatology, in which it is granted hospitality to what modern science, is the chromosome Cartesian: the doubt.

To understand the radical attitude of closing against each opposed hypothesis to the anthropogenic Global Warming, we think about the fact that, to avoid any discussion on this matter, the international scientific community chose to divide into two opposite "teams", the IPCC and the Nippc, that have the same goal, the secret of climate change, but they don't collaborate; They ignore each other.

The IPCC (Intergovernmental Panel on Climate Change) is an Intergovernmental Panel on Climate Change established in 1988. The working groups of the IPCC are the WMO (World Meteorological Organization) and UNEP (United Nations for the Environment Program) that study the Global Warming. All those did not share the thought of the IPCC have established the Nipcc (Nongovernmental Panel on Climate Change). It is outside of the Intergovernmental Panel but it consists of equally good scientists and scholars engaged in research like colleagues. The Italian Franco Battaglia is also a member of Nipcc. He is a professor of environmental physics and chemistry at the University of Modena; author of several publications about this theme.

The disproportion between the forces in the field (from funding and media point of view) is clear. This publication, however, wants to go beyond the conflict and offer a scientific alternative line of thought upon which to start a comparison free from prejudices and for this productive.

Our Planet is dynamic and has never been docile and not always benevolent towards its inhabitants, as well tell the mass extinctions that have occurred since the early days. Even today, our cities are based on huge clods of soil that float and move out of an incandescent magma, frequent source of great earthquakes and massive tsunami. The Theory of Madrigali invites you to be aware that the human race is master to improve or worse the living conditions of the Earth, but it can do little against natural forces and devastating events, including extreme climate changes.

Even climate, in fact, has its hidden energies that you can externalize with incredible rage. Thermal mutations, sudden, radical and prolonged are the order of the day in the Book of Time. So much so that we could say without fear of contradiction, after reading carefully the pages of the Book, that the thermal action of some recent hot decades is part of a climate process favorable to humanity. We must not be surprised in front of contingent events, looking for magical, supernatural explanations or improbable human origins, but rather we have to equip ourselves to predict them and to educate humanity to defend themselves.

Chapter I

History of climate

Look back to see what lies further ahead

The team of Meteo Mundi was borne with a task: study climate change and advance their knowledge with the aim of being able to predict as possible the occurrence, the duration and intensity of the phenomenology associated with them.

1.1. On the swing, from the mists of time

Analyzing past climate, we can observe a thermal provision aimed at an important climatic optimum towards the end of 1800 AD, after the Little Ice Age (very cold cycle started from 1400 AD) and with a significant acceleration and temporary fluctuations in the twentieth century, we have recorded a progressive increase towards the "optimal" to the end of the forties. In the fifties of the last century instead started a new cold period that lasted for about twenty–five years and ended in the eighties, when the average temperature started to rise again. During the twenty years eighties–nineties, finally, it was noted an acceleration of the hot, especially in the last decade. Only focusing on so limited period of time (one century) you can see a strong thermal mutability, which is always presented with repetitive rhythmic cadence each time, alternating warm cycles with periods of cooling.

1.2. 5,000 years ago: the ice melted, seas level up of 4 meters, escape from the Sahara

The interglacial age that we are living (and that is ending, now it is 11,500 years old) had a very hot period in its central part, between

5500 and 2400 BC, with temperatures much higher than the optimum of the Middle Ages. In that specific time, the ice melted and the seas level rose as much as 4 meters above the present level, while during the optimum of the Middle Ages (800–1200 AD), the limit of the seas rose from 50 centimeters to one meter, with the disappearance of iceberg. Also around 5000 BC one of the most welcoming and lush gardens of Planet turned into that vast desert area that now we call the Sahara: the few survivors migrated to the Nile delta, where they found favorable conditions to a great development. Egyptian civilization was born: Sphinx, pyramids and pharaohs are born, as many other pieces of human history, from a massive, cyclical and global climate change. Cores, in Antarctica and in the Arctic, but also by historical and archaeological campaigns, document these facts.

1.3. 600 years ago: the Little Ice Age

In 1200 A.D. a new "fresh" period starts and around 1400 A.D. the stiffer period of the climatic modern history starts, opening its doors to LIA (Little Ice Age). It is very cold season sharpened 1500 until 1870. Three hundred years in which, however, freezing winters alternated with occasional mild winters as well as perturbed summers (in greater numbers) to very hot summers. In short, even in the midst of a Little Ice Age, episodes of thermal contrast in those three and a half centuries were not lacking. Facts so obvious and so well documented in the past should at least tickle the curiosity of those interested in understanding the events of the present (and maybe of the future). Instead, the information of the climatic history of the Planet is scarce and little and nothing is done to rectify this serious gap. The historical aspect is ultimately been ignored or minimized, to credit the exceptional nature of the extreme hot of the recent past and in this way, validate an alleged process of anthropogenic warming. This ideological choice is distant, not only from the simple common sense (which sometimes deceives), but also and especially from a solid scientific thinking. If an event happened once can happen again, as common sense suggests. Even more if it has already happened several times.

1.4. Experience teaches, from the dictators to flood risk

The last two thousand years, for example, have shown that the advent of bloodthirsty dictators is not an extraordinary fact: Hitler and Stalin are just the latest (?) of a long series and for this reason, modern democratic states are trying save their constitutional systems from the looming danger (concrete) that the story certifies. They proclaimed "World Days of memory" to remember the facts and the predisposition to it with caution.

At this same principle adapts, or rather should adapt, a pillar of the scientific–technical planetary security related to the alleged vagaries of climate. We are talking about the so–called "flood risk".

The flood risk is the risk of flooding by water from natural or artificial streams. It is the product of two factors: the hazard (the probability of occurrence of a hazardous event of a certain size), and the expected damage (defined as loss of life or public and private economic assets).

The calculation of the flood risk is one of the hubs of each land–use planning. In according to it, in fact, those engineers, combining the data of intensity, duration, frequency and type of precipitation in a given geographical area with the capacity to contain water basins in that same area, establish if and how build bridges and other infrastructures to prevent rains and consequent floods that can destroy the area. The calculation of the flood risk establishes if, what, how much and how far it is possible to build around rivers, streams and lakes. The lives and property of entire communities, which must be kept away from these potential alluvial areas, depends on this calculation.

The laws in this area so delicate, in advanced countries, exist, but they never are quite strong and sometimes are flawed by a lack of memory. The assessment of the amount of rainfall expected, in fact, is often accomplished by analyzing statistics built on very small slices of the past, thirty, fifty or one hundred years at best. Once again, that we know "by the human memory".

The effects of this deficit are unfortunately evident. They build houses and factories where, in recent decades, all was right but one morning after a violent storm we have tragic scenarios caused by superficiality, or by speculative interest.

1.5. A lesson for everyone: the flood of 2012 in Tuscany

A demonstration of what we are saying comes from recent story: the disastrous flood that, in November of 2012, caused death and destruction (damage for hundreds and hundreds of millions of euros) in different areas of Tuscany, at the cities of Massa and Carrara to the southern part of the province of Grosseto, particularly in the town of Albinia.

In the night between 10th and 11th November, a scary amount of rainfall tumbled from the sky in a matter of a few hours. Authentic "water bombs" that caused literally the explosion of the streams and rivers. For this reason, in the aftermath, many people defined it as an "exceptional and unforeseeable event" and others used this catastrophe as proven evidence of tropicalizing of climate and consequently of Global Warming.

In the following weeks the experts, looking further back, realized that in the past in the area of Massa and Carrara phenomena like that had been occurred. One identical two hundred years before and another more violent than five hundred years before, but in any case when no anthropogenic pollution could have tickled climatic distortions whatsoever. It was not a "miracle", therefore, neither "unexpected exception", but only the repetition of a natural event not frequent. Its destructive effect is today amplified not by its uniqueness, but by the fact that around the rivers water has found things to be destroyed (entire towns) that did not exist before.

Therefore, during rebuilding, someone raised the issue of a revision of the calculation of flood risk, highlighting the necessity to parameterize again the danger of margins based on rainfall statistics considering the data of two–undren years at least.

In conferences organized throughout Italy and in schools, by disseminating on climate and exposing these issues, it is easy to note how the information in this field is absent or scarce. The common mistake that the public perceive, is have just an example, as point of reference, the last hot cycle where we lived the optimum in the temperate years between 1980–1990. This cycle is considered an exception and is motivated by the anthropogenic pollution. The human being does not have sufficient physical memory (we would need a few centuries of life more) to refute through his personal experience this empirical assumption. The empirical assumption ("never been so hot") becomes truth although in the Great Book of Time the extreme climate is a natural phenomenon and the temperature variations are part of a logic evolutionary that it is always presented with a rate defined.

Which is the danger of all this? We have seen it in the cited case (and it is not the only one) the recent floods in Tuscany: be unprepared in front of meteorological and climatic forces that drive our planet, which cyclically return to show their face darker and more violent.

The reading of the documents of the past, research and analysis of the oldest meteorological data, preserved in historical archives or obtained through coring and study of stratification, demonstrate the perennial thermal variability of the Planet, marked in cycles ranging from medium and short breaths (five–ten–twenty years) at longer times as secular and millennial intercession. It is a repetitive sequence of ice ages lasting about 100,000 years alternating with interglacial ages lasting about 11.000/11.500 years.

Careful studies on the Earth's climate history certifies this steady cadence, a periodic cadence, since it is always manifested and has always been respected over time as a process of thermic ups and downs which although varied is successive and uninterrupted.

Chapter II

Up there, in the control room

Who does control the climatic changes on Earth?

People proposed a lot of hypothesis about the cause of the cyclical and endless ice ages: why does the Earth freeze after a few of millennia?

2.1. The Sun and the orbital motions of the Earth? They are not important

The scholarly attention has focused on the simplest and rational answer: a periodic and traumatic decrease of the amount of solar heat on the planet. For a long time, in particular, they studied the orbital motions of the Earth, looking for regular intervals, which could explain the phenomenon.

The first and most important orbital motion observed was the revolution of the Earth around the Sun: an orbital plane (ecliptic)[1] that alternates from circular to elliptical, and shows in the aphelion its maximum radius (distance) from the nearest star (the Sun) and then, it takes place at the point of to the minimum distance: the perihelion. This variation range from elliptical to circular orbital is observed over a period of 100,000 years, with differences of solar energy in input supported by the minimum or maximum distance from the Sun. Other analyzed motion is the rotation of the planet on its axis that varies according to a tilt which changes in the periodic manner. This tilt of the Earth is responsible for the seasonal thermal variations between the solstices and equinoxes caused by the different inclination of the Sun to the individual latitudes and it marks the seasons. The axis

---

1. Ecliptic: circle up on the celestial sphere that corresponds to the apparent path of the Sun during the year.

oscillates with an angle that varies between a minimum of 22.1° (with controlled effect solstice, a less extreme, and more oceanic climate) to a maximum of 24.5° (characterized by a continental and more extreme climate). This process of oscillation of the axis between a minimum and a maximum ends in a time of about 41,000 years.

The precession of the equinoxes, with a cycle of about 21,500 years old, affects the position of Earth's axis, which undergoes a change due to the swelling gravitational axis Earth–Moon system. This gravitational force triggers a process that moves the axis of rotation Earth's fast, causing him to make a full turn. The effect of this astronomical phenomenon is a steady advance of the equinoxes, with variation of the distance between the Earth's orbital perihelion and aphelion, respectively distributed between the two hemispheres. This force changes the turnover of the seasons, with the result that in 10,000 years the axis will have a new orientation in the winter solstice. It will be positioned on the contrary, in the direction of the Star Vega and not to the Pole Star, promoting summer rather than winter. In other words, at 10,000 years, the minimum distance between the Earth and the Sun (perihelion) will no longer be in winter but in summer. Rotation of the Earth around the Sun, the Earth's axis oscillation, precession of the equinoxes: relevant orbital motions but they produce only small changes on the global solar input.

As it has been verified, the revolution of the Earth around the Sun induces a small thermal variation compared to the total annual quantity of energy and heat that the star sends to the Earth. The variation of the inclination of the axis and the precession only change the amount of energy distributed according to latitude, at a rate that produces oscillations of the seasonal distribution, but this does not involve significant alterations in total annual energy input from the Sun.

The three orbital motions examined by scholars, therefore, do not have significant effect on the total "amount" of heat that the Earth receives by the Sun; so the slight variations of input solar energy are not sufficient to explain climate change. On the other hand, it is shown that there is no phenomenon of decrease or increase in the source, as instead anyone has suspected. The amount of energy coming from the Sun is always the same, and in years of monitoring, satellites launched into orbit with the task of answering this specific question had never showed any significant changes in heat emitted by the Sun[2].

2.2. Finding the detonator

Soon our research has started looking for the "trigger", the really mechanism capable of activating the processes of global warming or cooling. We wanted to identify what leads the system to that point that marks the inevitable alternation between glacial and interglacial eras, regardless of the "classic" astronomical processes. The intuition was clear: an additional "force" still not taken into account by science had to exist that by acting on energy input and distributing it with the necessary modifications at different latitudes, it had the power to trigger the thermal variations detected during the climatic history of the Planet. It had to exists, because the "already explored" astronomical causes had been shown to cause minimal energy differences that were insufficient to determine important fluctuations of weather and climate. At the beginning, our attention is focused on other potentially crucial forces to the climate balance of the Planet. Gradually, however, we realized that these forces do not act independently, but they add up and interact with the principal force: the solar energy distributed at different latitudes. This complex interaction is the key to thermal variations recorded in every age and in every corner of the World.

2.3. Summers spark

A century ago, climatologists Croll and Milankovitch[3] had chosen the right path. Their theory put into the background classical astronomical variations to look for the "detonator", the cause of ignition of climate change. Croll identified it in a series of contiguous harsh winters;

---

2. Mario PINNA, *Le variazioni del clima*, Ed. Franco Angeli, Chap. 2, p. 46.

3. James CROLL (1821–1890): scottish scientist who developed the first theory of climate change based on changes in the Earth's orbit; Milutin MILANKOVIC (1879–1958): serbian climate scientist and engineer. *Studies with the cycles* (theory) is the theory of Milankovitch on climate change that have not yet concluded through changes in the movement of the Earth.

Milankovitch in a series of cooler and perturbed summers, with the increase of albedo effect, that is the relationship in percentage between the energy that arrives on Earth and the reflected energy in space with which the amount of solar heat that is "not absorbed" by the Earth is calculated[4].

The keystone of the whole process was near and the two prominent climate scientists had realized that the solution, the mechanism that governs the climate was not to be found in an alleged fluctuation of the energy coming from the Sun, but other contributing factors that change the distribution of that energy in different parts of the Earth. Today, the Madrigali Theory — Meteo Mundi confirms that pioneering insight: global climate change are the result of a combination of linked factors. One of these is certainly the variation of input solar energy, but it only is a factor of a physical, mathematical and astronomical wider context. A context in which the dominant role is played by the gravitational pull of the Moon and the Great general circulation of the atmosphere that uses, as "operational arm", a singular but powerful tool made of air and wind: the Jet Stream[5].

4. Albedo effect cited yet.
5. Jet Stream: Jet Stream–flow of air present in high altitude (from 5 to the limits of the tropopause) with fast flowing core of the jet just below the tropopause.

Chapter III

The power of the Jet Stream

The river of air that distributes the destiny of the World

Croll and Milankovitch were close to the heart of the enigma, but they could not dissolve it because a crucial piece was missing to their research: knowledge of the ways in which thermal energy is distributed at different latitudes of the Planet through the Great general circulation of the atmosphere. Instead, Madrigali Theory identifies this element. Croll and Milankovitch, even if they had produce divergent conclusions, they had not wrong to attach great importance to the phenomenon of special seasonal events that trigger a relevant process of cooling or heating through a succession of metelogical and thermal events particularly persistent.

These the thermal and meteoric strategic changes depend on the Grande general circulation and on the Jet Stream, which determines them with specific and repetitive rhythms. The Jet Stream plays a decisive role in climate change. What is it?

3.1. The intuition of Top Gun

This gaseous fluid, which is between 5 and 12 kilometers altitude, was discovered during the Second World War, when American pilots flying up and down from Hawaii casually crossed it. Traveling at high altitude, pilots encountered heavy turbulence, despite the weather reports said the contrary. The reports had always gaven time stable for air navigation and guaranteed the absence of flight problems, but who was on board had problems. Pilots, suspicious by such discrepancy and worried by frequent difficulties that they have to face, have deepened the matter and have discovered the existence of this tropospheric current.

The airflow is not a "breeze" but rather is comparable to a giant highway air, with a diameter of 400 kilometers, thickness between 5 and 12 km and incalculable length, extending for thousands of miles. This colossal "conveyor belt", so called for its thermal balancing and distributor nature of air masses that move around the Earth, through the hemispheres of the Planet from west to east, with variable speed between a minimum of 80 and up to 250 kilometers per hour.

The research on which is based Madrigali Theory has made evident the invasive strong power of the tropospheric flow from the metereological point of view, clarifying with extreme precision as the Jet Stream is able to shape and trigger each thermal event.

3.2. The lord of the winds and currents

The current has a fundamental role in the marine surface circulation. In fact it controls the dominant of the movement of surface flows, triggered by the process of "scraping" of the "dominant" winds on the ground that are controlled by the flow of tropospheric flood, which constantly interact on the surface of the oceans.

Typical examples of this cause and effect relationship are the trade winds that blow in Northeast > South–West direction in the northern hemisphere and in Southeast > Northwest direction in the Southern Hemisphere. They are generated by mathematical–physical causes established by the Great the general circulation of the atmosphere.

Another example (but we could do this on any surface sea current) is the Gulf Stream that following in Southwest > Northeast direction mitigates the climate of some European nations. In fact, compared to Canada and North America, which are located on the same northern latitudes, Europe has less extreme temperatures. The activity of the Jet Stream requires the westernization of the oceanic flow, leading to the climatic situation that we have just outlined.

The investigation on the Jet Stream has marked a further step forward in the definition of the climate Great Machine and its role. It shows that the incoming solar energy (invariable) has a specific task: providing fuel to the entire machine and that the Jet Stream is the responsible of diffusion of air masses, between the various latitudes.

This determines, depending on how will the current altitude, temperature differences among major areas of the World that are placed on the same parallel, where the Sun's energy should be uniform.

One of the best–known cases is the huge climate disparity that exists between the city of Naples (Italy) and New York (USA), in spite of latitude shared. This difference can be explained only by identifying a force that, independently of the energy input from the Sun, is able to distribute this energy in different ways in the same latitude. This force is the Jet Stream.

The Jet Stream has a very high decision–making role in the glaciological variations. The depth analysis on the persistence of the current certifies that the Jet Stream determines the variation of albedo effect on the Earth's surface and reinforces those effects of cooling or heating which are the basis to establishing significant bearing thermal cycles. In the middle of the last century, also Hurd Curtis Willett (1903–1992) a U.S. climatologist noted the importance of the Great general circulation of the atmosphere for the terrestrial climate change. Willet highlighted the strategic importance of the great polar vortex at high altitude (pV), classifying it as an essential element in the atmospheric circulation at high latitudes. He had guessed that this phenomenon was able to change the disposition of the centers of high and low pressure to tropospheric altitudes, and consequently to the large air masses.

In the eighties of the past century, Hermann Flohn and Karl W. Butzer[1] took up this theory but they did not develop it probably because it went against the theory of anthropogenic Global Warming that in those years was consolidating.

3.3. It is summer's fault

To understand the relevance of this research path, we must take a step back and return to Croll and Milankovitch. According to Croll the winter season is the primary cause of a possible change in thermal

---

1. Hermann FLOHN (1912–1997): meteorologist and climatologist. Karl W. BUTZER environmental archaeologist and ecological culture, american geographer has a master in meteorology and geography. For the complete historical reconstruction should read *Mario Pinna and "climate change"*, Chap. 3, p. 65.

addressed to a gradual cooling process. This is due to the combined effect of constant succession of harsh winters, with deposit of snow on the ground and on continents resulting an increased albedo effect. For Milankovitch, instead, the key period to explain the initiation of new climatic cycles is summer. According to the Croatian scholar, what amplifies the process of heat exchange is not as significant a harsh winter, but a number of cool and disrupted summers in which the process of sublimation of snow is less. More snow on the mountains and still greater reflectivity of the clouds leads to an increase in the albedo and thus a lowering of the average global temperature. Our research confirms the importance of Croll and Milankovitch findings: concomitant season action, supporting in particular, by the theory of Milankovitch on summer season.

The comparison of various data, historical documents related to meteorological situations, ice cores and the Jet Stream in the past, highlights the importance of the summer. The intersection and overlap of this information reveal that the cooling process is the result of abnormal and perturbed or extremely dynamic summers such as "slow down" the process of sublimation of snow and feed the progression of glaciers. The summer season is a key factor from the standpoint of climate, because it can balance the effect of a very rigid winter, it also is the possible ignition spark of an important thermal change.

This analysis must be applied on a global level and not on local level where there are frequent, contradictory effects that leading to make errors in the assessment. We will explain in detail this aspect of the problem, analyzing the "micro–climates". For example in the Mediterranean area: here, the atmospheric events occurred in recent years should be interpreted in a broader process. In particular, thermal situations, that they opposed to the process of global cooling in place (which we will fully realize later), are specific effects of the extension of Jet Stream to–wards the ground on this particular geographic latitude.

We know that a cooling cycle starts from the northern latitudes and it expands to southward, moving from altitude to the ground. In southern latitudes, the Mediterranean ones, the alarm bell rings at high altitude, on the reliefs. These are directly exposed to tropospheric flow, where we can detect an overall cooling; in particular by monitoring the evolution of glaciers and permafrost[2]. The glaciers and permafrost on the Gran Sasso massif, in the heart of south central Italy and the Mediterranean area, are trying to expand and consolidate themselves it is a clear example in this sense.

The Mediterranean area enjoys a specific climate, encased in a basin of water protected by the Alps and influenced by the proximity of the hottest African continent. Despite its convenient location, it inevitably succumbs to temperature changes triggered by the global Jet Stream of the free atmosphere. Symptoms of cooling in a close to the sea can be less violent and less explicit than elsewhere, but the diagnosis is done at high altitude, and it says that the "cold" is coming.

The Great general circulation of the atmosphere remains the *dominus* of the situation. Thanks to its action, summer season is the key to the global climate balance. For example, if the Jet Stream develops prevailing processes of long–term stability, attracting air masses to high temperatures, it increases dryness and encourages sunshine. This, inevitably, causes the reduction of the snow and suffering of the glaciers with a consequent decrease of albedo effect.

We have the opposite effect if a dominant feature of the insistence of JS to degenerative weather situations, recalling colder air masses that trigger the cooling action on the continents. This phase induces a pejorative action (bad weather and recall of polar or arctic air), with the construction of cloud cover and snowfall that tend to grows up the expansion of glaciers and encourage an increase of albedo effect. The result is a gradual cooling process.

Cloudiness and heavy snowfall are the main responsible for the birth, maintenance and development of glaciers. An increased presence of snow and glaciers develops the high reflectivity of the Sun's rays, thus emphasizing the phenomenon of albedo. The consequence is the start of a sublimation[3] process of the residual snow that it means the passage of the snow from solid to vapor state.

We can mistakenly think that a dye–sublimation process is accelerated by warmer winters. In fact, the responsible is not a mild winter

2. Permafrost: present at the poles as in the high mountains, it is a land where the soil is permanently frozen for at least 2 years.

3. Sublimation: phase transition from solid to gaseous state.

(where the snow equally falls at high latitudes as well as at mountains) but a very hot and dry summer.

This climate element, which is balanced by a cooling and heating periods, it builds and breaks for a decisive action of atypical and cadence persistence operated by the Great general circulation of the atmosphere. Through the Jet Stream, it produces precise exchanges of warm and cold air masses to the different latitudes.

The intersection of statistical data and physical–mathematical process shows that there is a correlation between the changes triggered by specific actions in the Grand general circulation of the Atmosphere and its persistence effect on certain geographical areas. This is decisive, because the Jet Stream activity is able to create thermal and meteorological effects until to produce significant degenerative changes, which always start from high altitudes, and then they distribute themselves to the ground with intense and persistent effects.

Madrigali Theory — Meteo Mundi analyzes and explains all cause–effect relationship outside the known astronomical influences, with the intention to deepen and highlight the role of a climatic power: the Jet Stream. This one is a strategic aspect of mathematical and physical nature that interacting with a physical–astronomical phenomenon (gravitational lunar force) that influences the weather and climate of the World. The "real responsibility" of large thermal events succeeded on Earth over the millennia is here, always alternating in time and space.

The tropospheric flow (Jet Stream) establishes, with its relentless action, the weather patterns, the atmospheric behavior during the days, and the climatological one; it means statistical rhythm of the weather events during the months, years, decades and centuries.

3.4. Caught in the Vortex

The close relation between Jet Stream and climate change shows more than a mere intuition by analyzing the different angle of sunlight on the soil of the globe, which creates the gap between the thermal Pole (deficit) and the equator (excess). This phenomenon generates two important motor centers of cold air positioned on the Poles: the Arctic and Antarctic vortices. Two essential figures, which play a role in the penetration of cold air to the South, driven by Nature to balance the large temperature difference that exists between the polar latitudes and equatorial–tropical ones.

The Arctic vortex is a depression on the boreal northern latitudes, consisting by a circulation with western cold features. A thermal anticyclone with northeast winds that tends to be stationed on the ground; a hothouse of arctic air, which is driven by the polar vortex to the mid–low latitudes.

This dynamic structure of the artic Jet Stream reveals its seasonal evolution: expanding winter caused by the increased contribution of cold air in the shadow hemisphere, and contraction in the summer caused by the opposed solar activity that involves the hemisphere where we find a lot of light in this season.

The seasonal variation encourages the two separate periods of light, respectively marked by the great night and the great day, which occur in the two Poles. With the start of the hot and cold semester, marked by the entrance of the equinoxes with the peak of solstices, the classic meteorological evolution takes place on a global scale.

3.5. Watch out for waves!

The Jet Stream in the free atmosphere remains divided into two separate streams. A main branch that marks the birth of the polar front, at a height of 10 km and variable latitude between $40°$ and $65°$ in winter and in summer, and the sub–tropical branch, active between 13 and 14 km of altitude, depending on the season, between $25°$ and $40°$ of latitude.

These two jets, strategic for the fate of weather and climate of the entire Planet, have in winter, for the larger thermal contrasts, a lower altitude and an increased speed, with a trajectory of moving closer to the equator. In summer, the lower thermal contrast, caused by heat, pushes the jets at higher levels and decreases speed of making them retire towards the poles.

Research conducted over the last decades has found, in this constant "back and forth movement" of the Jet Stream, a substantial differences between the winters of the '60s and '70s, those of the optimum '80–'90 and the cycle of the new trend of the year 2000. It clearly shows that the variations triggering short–medium and long–term tropospheric flow, and not the seasonal cycles, decide and influence these changes, global weather, climate.

The careful observation of the Great general circulation of the atmosphere and the Jet Stream showed a repetitive cycle of oscillation. This periodicity is marked by precise configurative mathematical–physical movements with effects of persistence and phenomenology, which varies between three and five weeks, controlled and regulated by the Moon's gravitational force and identified by the vector sums of the forces in play.

The process starts from a maximum of the flow velocity, which gradually decreases, then dissolves, and returns to form a new period of evolution. A flow that can occurs on the same areas (the phenomenon of persistence) or it carries on adjacent points (new cycles of persistence).

The stream has a lilting evolution and reaches a maximum speed of 250 km / h straight, with only modest undulations. This phase marks a baric evolution called "high zonal index", and is the typical western oceanic flow. When its speed drops below 150 km / h, the component of the tropospheric flow becomes more undulating and organizes itself with various waves of the concerned hemisphere. These waves are crucial for the "climate" because they are warmer to the northern latitudes and colder to south, with a jet that descends invading lower latitudes.

When the speed is lowered further, down to below 70 km / h, the half–waves slow down and come with deep corrugations of different width. These waves determine perturbed action depending on their arrangement (ample waves disrupted weather with quick passages, narrow waves perturbations of greater intensity and slow progression).

If the flow reaches a top speed of propagation, called "critical value" of the Rossby wave[4] propagation (the half–wave was called Rossby from discover name) we have a substantial change in the jet. We observe that formation of flow propagation is not zonal, but sundial, which can also makes a "no zonal" moving, from east to west with air masses propagation coming from the east. This evolution is very

---

4. Wave of Rossby: planetary waves with twists and turns made by Jet Stream, researched and discovered by Carl Gustaf Rossby (1898–1957), swedish meteorologist.

critical for Europe and the Mediterranean, because it identifies the standard conducive configuration to the spread of cold air masses from Siberia.

Often with the onset of the critical value with minimum speed of propagation, we have the fracture of the jet, with the disposition of closed waves with a circulation hourly: a warmer air clockwise, counter–clockwise disrupted air with more cold mass.

These standing waves, which are formed by a fracture of the flow, are of considerable relevance climate, because they have often a block evolved (persistence). The baric evolution called "open" occurs when they occur in a context of the Jet Stream with a branch of the bypass flow, but always fed by cold air. They can also evolve into a training configurative called "closed" (cut–off–standing wave) where the circulation is cut off from the main jet and is no longer supplied by the principal tropospheric current.

A "heavy" evolution in terms of climate for its weather effects that produce a constant phenomenology. In this particular phase, it can induce an atmospheric persistence able to reach thermal meteoric extreme limits.

These figures of high and low pressure manifest as closed waves that reproduce various fractures of the jet and may recur with a frequency in the same latitudes. Typical evolution, which sharpens a precise meteorological effect of repetition on the ground. The repetitively of Jet Stream can vary between dry and warm cycles with thermal values over the average, and cold periods of intense rain or snow with unusual temperatures.

It is important to say that these baric figures are essential to the terrestrial heat balance, because they are used by the Great general circulation of the atmosphere to transporting air masses at different latitudes. In this way, it reaches thermal equilibrium sought by the nature of the circulation of cold air masses at South and movements of warm air masses to the north, to balance the thermal gap existing between the Poles and the Equator–Tropics.

Solar energy supplies the fuel (engine) to tropospheric flow and its inexhaustible "motor activity", but the input motion to whole complex climate weather, approaching the Madrigali Theory, comes from the Moon vector forces (gravitational) who interact with the air mass of the Great General Circulation of atmosphere.

The dynamic of the atmosphere has a complex but fascinating process. To make understandable to anyone the basic principle, it suffice say that the provision of divergence at high altitude, which controls all processes in the Jet Stream, the weather changes and global climate, distinguishes the atmospheric pejorative aspect, the convergence and the opposite effect as stabilizer. The creation of negative stabilizing and positive degenerative cyclonic vortices also plays an important role in the formation at high altitudes.

3.6. Dangerous rotations

We have already said a lot about of this continuous flow of air, the Jet Stream, comparing it among other things. As motorway, the Jet Stream has two directions: it often runs along the zonal western, that is oriented from west to east, but sometimes it makes "an inversion of lane" and it takes the opposite direction when the flow reverses its course and becomes no zonal, moving from east to west.

This "full rotation" of the flow assumes utmost importance from the meteorological point of view because it is a determining factor on the effects of climate at precise geographical latitudes. For example, the Euro–Mediterranean area, where the retrograde (east to west) conveys cold air masses (much colder than normal sea currents Western) that usually in winter stationed on the Russian–Siberian lowlands. The inversion of the motion is caused by the critical point of wave propagation (the so–called Rossby waves) in the flow and it generates this particular eastern expansion of winds of high altitude that, in winter, also dramatically cools part of the European Union, including the Mediterranean. Analyzing the stiffer winter cycles registered in Europe, we will always find a concomitant retrograde flow of the Jet Stream, with cold Eastern currents able, in some cases, to resemble the Mediterranean, from the climatic point of view, to Scandinavia.

Miracles of the Jet Stream. His power of action is until now taken inexplicably in little consideration. A power that does not end here.

The Jet Stream has a strategic importance for all weather events in Nature. However, it is also used by the air navigation and to facilitate flights to save fuel.

This huge air flow has the specific task of transporting the excess thermal energy to different latitudes, inserted in the depths of the Great general circulation of the atmosphere.

If Planet did not rotate on itself, the Great general circulation of the atmosphere would have a substantially less complex direction, divided into two main motor centers : a thermal convection mega cell of heat in equatorial latitudes and descending at polar latitudes. The excess of heat on the equatorial belt, caused by the more direct sunlight action, would be recalled at high latitudes by mega cell convective equatorial and favored by the hot air would rise with up–ward motions until to reach the Poles with subsequent downward motion. The warmer air descent falling would push the cooler air mass, that stationing at the Poles to the lower latitudes, forming a reverse current of cooling from Poles to Equator, so closing the circuit obtaining the thermal equilibrium. In this way, we would have the perfect thermal balance in every latitude of the globe, compensating for the energy surplus generated by the different inclination of the solar rays at different latitudes. Science defines it as "circulation theory".

In reality, the concrete mechanism of energy transport is very different from the theory. It is complicated by the Earth's rotation on its axis. This rotation generates a flow deviation to the right in the northern hemisphere and to the left to Southern Africa, triggered by the law of Coriolis' force[5], with fragmentation and division of the flow into cells that are three: Hadley cell[6], equatorial and tropical, the Ferrel one of mid–latitude, and Hadley at polar latitudes. Three cells that form autonomous atmospheric circulations at high altitude.

The three distinct circulations interacting with intersections of contact between the various jets; and it is precisely here, in the points of contiguity of altitude, where the process "sorting" of energy happen: the process of deploying of heat at different latitudes, but in a very inhomogeneous way, with striking differences of atmospheric effect.

These differences in the effect of Great general circulation of atmo-

5. Law of Coriolis: apparent force to which a body is subjected when it is observed in a reference system of circular motion with respect to an inertial reference frame, caused by the rotation of the planet, it is maximum at Poles and null at equator. Discoverer Guspard–Gustave de Coriolis (1792–1843).

6. Cells Hadley / Ferrel: type of atmospheric circulation typically convective–lawyer and scholar of English meteorology (1685–1768).

sphere are related to the nature of jets (thermal) and to incidence of flows (stable / unstable and persistence), which tend to diversify even at the same latitude. This explains the complexity of "real" climatic mechanism, able to generating very different situations in the areas, with showy effects also along the same parallel.

Madrigali Theory and Meteo Mundi Project study the diversification of tropspheric flow at different latitudes that, distributed in time and space, develops egregious variations able to affect the weather and climate on the ground.

Chapter IV

A walk in the microclimates

Observe the "local" to avoid "global" blunders

Before getting to the heart of the Meteo Mundi research, we have to do some valuable "meterological reflections". This issue was born from the observation of detailed sequence of weather events, in diachrony, and in synchrony; in relation to the study of microclimates.

The Earth's thermal mechanism is much more complex than you might imagine. Its evolution proves completely released by the presence of human beings, who have a definitely irrelevant power to the thermal fate of the Earth. The man has only the power to interact (and only) with microclimates (urban centers), but not in a way to govern the climate of the Planet, whose underlying cause remains the Nature.

4.1. Urban distortions

The microclimates are definitely very important for a proper weather forecasting, but they are always constrained by the presence of the Great general circulation of the atmosphere.

The localized climate or microclimate is the occurrence of thermal and weathering interaction processes that tend to enhance or inhibit a specific atmospheric process in specific geographical locations and spatial conformations: the presence of mountain ranges, valleys, and lakes, proximity to sea, typology and morphology of the territory. The microclimate is not process caused by the anthropogenic intervention, whose typical example is urbanization, constantly expanding with increase of urban areas at the expense of green and consequent exaltation of albedo effect.

Now, we will back to the problem of influence (almost imperceptible) of anthropic action on global climate. We can take in exam, for example, the case of the so–called continental climate.

The continental climate, as it is known, brings out the extreme heat that is manifested by substantial differences in temperature between on average very cold winter and very hot summer. A phenomenon caused by the remoteness of surface sea, which tends to erode the thermal extremes.

Let us look at the city of Florence, in Tuscany, urban and continental area where there are significant extremes of temperature. These seasonal differences, even egregious, are precisely generated by the distance of the city center from the sea. The topography of the area further emphasizes thermal fluctuations: a basin (plain) surrounded by hills and mountains that prevent proper ventilation.

The presence of stagnant air on a plain surrounded by mountains with small elevation tends to worsen the temperature inversion, further accentuated by the presence of a significant urbanized area. The process of building and thinning of the existing vegetation, an expansive extension of the suburbs, affects thermal extremes, both to the "hot" than to the "cold", for contributing factors dependent on the percentage values of albedo. This climatic effect does not affect the overall average temperatures, neither local nor global. Ones again it is determined by the action of the Jet Stream.

In urban areas, the temperature extremes have been strengthen, just a few degrees. This peculiarity, however, is intimately linked to the evolutionary process of the Jet Stream in the free atmosphere. Ground temperatures, even in the urbanized territory, affected by specific thermal variations constrained by the type of air mass (polar and subtropical) callback to all units, built and distributed by the tropospheric flow on the basis of equally specific physical–mathematical causes. The physical process (thermal) found on urban areas only detects exaltation of extremes, however, that never takes the character of anthropogenic prevaricating action.

The important factor is the nature of the incoming air mass and its persistence over time. In this sense, studies have found that with the advent of afro–Mediterranean air mass, temperatures will increase for the contribution of Saharan warm. We will say the same, on the contrary, for the interference of cold continental masses, which are to emphasized the process of heat loss by nocturnal radiation accentuated by thermal inversions.

The presence of the agglomeration enhances the continentally of the microclimate, but it cannot play a decisive role in the variations of the average global temperature. It can, we are at a crucial point, produces a serious perspective mistake, that not change numbers, but their analysis and interpretation from a global point of view.

The presence of edification and anthropogenic influence in general, alters the reading of climatic data. In cities, particularly if very large, the concreting enhances thermal effect, but with scraps of values detected both upwards and downwards. We do not register a thermal progressive action generated by human intervention (and in particular by the introduction of CO_2 in the air), but simply a localized effect linked to the presence of the urban agglomeration.

4.2. If the station tricks

Surveys and audits of the meteorological stations of the old urban location confirm an obvious contamination of statistical data. This fact is caused to the variations of thermal energy, which are enhanced by the presence of cement and asphalt where previously there were fields or trees. The average temperature detected in urbanized centers should be verified and monitored more carefully, to avoid build "spoiled" data on the reading of the annual average. The professional weather stations would place, installed in accordance with WMO[1], in selected areas, far from cities and not influenced by external factors. In short, a temperature that should be used to formulate a climate statistics must necessarily be detected following functional principles to the elaborate a real statistic, using weather stations located in uncontaminated areas.

To clarify this aspect, that is apparently marginal but in reality is a decisive concept, we observe another microclimate, well known to the writer, the city of Grosseto, in Tuscany, an area of lowland (called Maremma) that extends around an urban agglomeration with maritime influence to the west and continental one to east.

---

1. World Meteorological Organization.

The hills surround the Maremma plain, which is open to the west towards the Tyrrhenian Sea and the Tuscan Archipelago. In this vast area, until the mid–twentieth century virtually untouched and partly swampy, in recent decades a strong process of urbanization has been produced, which is still in place. The results is a progressive reduction of clearing and pasture to make room for overbuilding that exacerbates continental climate. The proliferation of buildings and roads multiplies the effect of the high power heating and cooling just like cement and bitumen, accentuating the differences in seasonal temperature.

In this last decade, we have recorded divergent values for some Celsius degrees compared to those that the plain natural offered previously, before the urbanization. In winter Grosseto revealed an average lower temperature than the past one, in the presence of cold air with thermal inversions exalted by periods of high pressure and air stagnation; on the other hand, in summer it is warmer for the consequences of urbanization that "continentalizes" the climate and reinforces the extremes. In any case, the alternation of the seasons produces these increases and decreases, resulting, in the context of annual, only appreciable difference respect to the past, but that is insufficient to suggest an anthropogenic cause for climate change.

The air masses moving and their persistence over time can reveal the origin of climate change. To understand it, the observation of air masses of reference that generated the cause–and–effect corresponding to specific thermal meteoric actions is essential. The analysis of these data taken from weather up to standard, professional and controlled stations, allowing us to identify the work of the tropospheric flow and its importance in the processes of climate change, prevaricating on the limited effects of interaction with a specific geographical and weak anthropic contribution conveyed by the interference of a generic urban agglomeration.

It is evident that the importance to have statistical data correctly compiled and the need to adapt, for this purpose, the professional weather stations now encompassed by urban expansion. The stations are the basis of a solid scientific research on climate change, which is the element to prevent that the increase of average temperatures is not to be caused by real climate change but by numbers instrumentation.

Studying the climate change is essential to determine the physical–mathematic cause of the thermal process detected. The thermal average is heavily affected, more than in any other factor, by the transit characteristics of specific air mass in arrival (arctic/polar or subtropical) and by their persistence and consequent cyclicity. This applies to any corner of the planet, to every latitude and longitude.

In contrast to the current dominant thought, that attaches to the human activity a decisive impact on global climate change, Madrigali Theory and Meteo Mundi Project reveal the marginal power of anthropogenic action on climate, except local implications related to urbanization.

4.3. The whole truth on the CO_2

The same air pollution threat, tangible and concrete to human health, not plays a significant role in the drama of climate upheavals: variations in the levels of CO_2 in the atmosphere have always expressed, in the long history of Earth, and in a dramatic way.

The topic is the most debated; Mario Pinna[2] in his study whit a completeness of information confirms important oscillations of the CO_2 over the millennia.

The examination of air bubbles trapped in the layers of ice in Greenland and Antarctica, which started in 1980, has allowed us to detect the percentages of CO_2 and through these have had precise answers that are in contradiction to the theory of Global Warming.

In the period of glacial cooling, the concentration of the gas was in sharp drop, while it tended to rise, also drastically, in heating periods. This data confirms that striking variations in the concentration of CO_2 occurred also in remote past, in the absence of any anthropogenic action.

The glacial stratigraphy performed in Antarctica has offered an impressive amount of data which confirm how the variations of the CO_2 does not adversely affect the temperature, but they are a later immediately consequence of thermal effect. It demonstrates how the concentration of carbon dioxide and the temperature are swinging, upwards or downwards, both still lagging behind with respect to the radiation. In cooling processes, for example, first radiation decreases,

---

2. Mario PINNA, *Climate Variations*, Chap., 2 p. 54.

then the CO_2 and temperature degrease too; but the deflection of the carbon dioxide takes place immediately after that of the temperature!

The stratigraphy reinforces the idea that the CO_2 gives a positive feedback to the processes of glaciation and deicing, but does not represent a politicking mechanism.In other words, the CO_2 variations appear a direct consequence of the thermal variations and not a root cause of this, as many scientific communities have assumed in these decades.

Moreover, CO_2 is a vital gas to the planet, and not only because it is decisive element in the vital process of photosynthesis. If there were no carbon dioxide, in fact, the overall cooling would be unstoppable and would condemn the Earth to live with temperatures much lower than the current.

CO_2 is crucial for the greenhouse effect, which reduces the loss of reflected energy from the Planet toward space. It is essential in the "composition" of the microclimates, to analysis its presence and to formulate a trusted localized forecast. To understand the origin of the climatic changes we must look elsewhere, to specific masses of air in arrival and to the Jet Stream configuration.

4.4. Heaven and Earth Effect

Back to microclimates, in addition to CO_2 there are other collateral factors to consider for a correct interpretation of the vagaries of the specific weather. Among these, the presence of the ridges, which exalt the internal hilly plains because the orographic barrier prevents the penetration of oceanic air (sea). In the same way, but with the opposite effect, the mountains stop cold air masses directed toward oceanic places, limiting cold in some areas than others, even with the same latitude. Typical example, in this sense, the Mediterranean basin, which is protected to the north by the Alps.

In mountainous areas, the rainfall is fostered on windward slopes, for the ascent forced of the moist air, which causes cooling, and condensation. This peculiarity linked to the specific geography of the territory is the cause of rainfall and flood. But they are extreme, once again, only in persistence of the Jet Stream.

In the presence of flow wet disturbed, mountain slopes and hilly areas, exposed to the action of closing up on the windward side of moist air, are more rainy than leeward ones, effect accentuated by any marine surfaces or lakes close to the projections. The moisture and condensation contribution is considerably higher and rainfalls are concentrated, active and abundant.

The study on weather and climate in areas characterized by the presence of mountains and water basins (seas or lakes), confirms, with indisputable evidence, the importance of tropospheric flow. The microclimates are interesting from the meteorological point of view, because they can enhance a process of thermal and meteoric interference; depend on primary force for excellence: the Jet Stream of the free atmosphere, *dominus* of climatic variations on the Earth.

The force of tropospheric flow makes extreme and/or changes the climatic context on a large scale. The observation of the flow reveals a constant variation in its evolution that is made available with certain pressure configurations at altitude, ranging from 5 to 12 km altitude.

These changes of direction, speed and persistence change the meteorological and climate framework, affecting any microclimate. This degenerative process can could be joined to extreme situations and encourage mighty and devastating phenomena as floods, flooding, strong winds, frosty air and torments of snow, or on the contrary, extreme heat, persistent stability, low rainfall and drought.

Madrigali Theory concentrated for years on meticulous study about the Jet Stream of the free atmosphere, had to look for in this tropospheric river: a long journey of research in the "heart" of the great general circulation of the atmosphere and in its arrangement, and in its interior element, the Jet Stream.

Chapter V

No climate no weather forecast

The inexplicable divorce of two genetically conjugated sciences
a network to bring them together in marriage

We observed, as the climatic changes important, be they local or global, are the direct consequence of meteorological phenomena particular and persistent, and induced in turn by the action of the great general circulation of the atmosphere by means of the Jet Stream.

However, there is a lot of confusion around the concepts of meteorology and climatology, many consider as two separate sciences. In reality, however, are cohesive and concatenated.

Meteorology is the science that deals with investigating and predicting weather events (thermal and meteoric) during the days. The observation of meteorological data, their succession and their monthly, yearly and ten–yearly development is the basis of the climatology, which analyzes meteorological events (atmospheric) over the course of time (years, decades, centuries).

The evidence is that cannot exist a study on climate not compared it to the observation (meteorological) of the thermal events and weather. It is a serious mistake analyzing climate statistics and ignoring the cause–effect from which have been generated.

The intercession of the great general circulation of the atmosphere and, in fact, the cause which imparts, for the different intrusion of the air in transit masses, those thermal effects on such as, detected over the years, builds the statistical database of world averages.

Climatology is obliged to know meteorology and evaluation of weather events, which have occurred over time, because only this accurate vision can help him to carry out its statistic tasks. It is essential compare the data examined both from meteorological that statistic the point of view; only in this way is it possible to ascertain if this data are correct, wrong or disguised. Only in this way it is possible understand the jet arrangement and the causes of the effects it produces.

5.1. Nonsense: myopic sentinels

The weather survey network with various monitoring stations has a fundamental role for the meteorological and climate correct identification. The climate statistic is punctuated by configurative trends of the great general circulation of the atmosphere, with the atmospheric and thermal changes in the course of time triggered and regulated by precise arrangement of tropospheric flow and by its extreme variability.

Only a legal standard weather station can make a precise atmospheric analysis revealing the direct consequence, in the ground, of the downward projection of the Jet Stream location. An exact meteorological analysis with an installed, monitored and controlled network of weather station identifies the correspondence of effect in projection from high altitudes of the atmosphere toward the low atmospheric layers. A network of detection may not only be used as climate statistic, but it should be inserted in a broader context of work and research aimed to identify the real tropospheric conditions. For this reason, it is essential that any errors in data provided by obsolete or not under WMO law, stations must be carefully removed, at least from statistical computation.

We will describe later in detail in chapter 10, the project Meteo Mundi for the installation of a detection network able of providing reliable data according to WMO international law. This project utilizes the technical advice of Pierluigi Caruso, technology manager of Weather Mundi and describes the whole plan of installation of a network of weather high technology stations in various parts of the world. We will limit now reiterating the decisive point of the matter: a network of weather stations and professional to the cutting edge of technology is essential. It is the only capable of monitoring and studying the behavior of the dynamics of the atmosphere (Jet Stream) and thus offer scientific responses to the enigma of the climatic changes. The climate statistics is formed by the archive of weather events detected by weather stations, we have to understand that incorrect data and findings undermine every possible interpretation and research on climate.

Often occurred the obsolescence of the networks of weather stations, with the consequent high error rates caused by lack of adequate maintenance of stations and of the necessary operations of sensors calibration.

5.2. Looks blurred on a limited horizon

The World Meteorological Organization establishes that for each station average climatological values has to be calculated, related to rainfall with the maximum and minimum temperatures, based on the average data derivable from observations made in thirty years of climate reference between 1961 to 1990. This parameter is the reference medium with which they are compared the data of observed temperatures with daily monthly and annual reports, on thermal situation and on rainfall.

Considering the trend of the average global temperature of the Earth is also true that about two–thirds of the years taken to reference have been characterized for mean lower values than those of previous decades, than following decade and the current. This fact is opening a debate among scholars about a possible change in the sense of an extension, period of time average climate reference.

It seems possible have doubts on the prevalent anthropogenic theory on climate change; the data on the recent global warming would be corrupted by does not complete and homogeneous distribution of weather stations on the globe, or for the modification of the surrounding environment (from rural and urban) in which these stations are located, undergoing the called "heat island" effect.

For this reason this project is very important; it wants give scientific credibility to the first element of every possible research: numbers.

5.3. Holidays in the Sahara: when the arithmetic gives the numbers

On this aspect, namely the need to use with maximum caution concept of average thermal and the related statistics, the same Mario Fin was already very clear. Flipper writes:

It is appropriate to remember, that the temperature is a quality of atmosphere and not a physical quantity in the strict sense of the term. This means that the numeric values with which we usually express the temperature could not add or multiply as subtract each other, for example, say that a certain temperature of 10°, if added to another 5°, from a value of 15° has not sense. It happens that the climate scientist makes similar operations researching the average values; for example, when he sums the temperatures read on the thermometer for every single hour and then divides result for 24 to obtain the daily average. These operations are considered only as necessary calculations to obtain a result, being devoid of any physical meaning.[1]

An impeccable enunciation, which stresses as a purely arithmetic is, by its nature, empirical and susceptible to serious shortcomings, useless to indicate important climatic variations.

To understand how much the simple thermal average has little to say on the actual climate "quality", we only make a simple example. Imagine ask your travel agent a nice vacation in a place in the world in which the average daily temperature is 20 degrees centigrade, in short, the ideal temperature. The agent, with arithmetic averages in hand, will have no doubts and will take you on holiday in the Sahara desert, where during the day it goes above 40 degrees and at night it drops below zero!

The mathematic average can have a function strongly indicative only in the detection of the temperatures in the equatorial band, where there is not the phenomenon of the thermal excursion. Here, in fact, any important variations of the average would be significant, indicating, especially if it is prolonged and constant, a real tendency toward the hot or cold.

At the Equator, in spite of all the anguish of the theoreticians of the Global Warming, we record nothing: a flat average, always, without changing.

Therefore, a first problem is giving to statistical averages, compared to limited reference period, a decisive "specific weight" because in reality, they do not have the identification of global climate change. In fact, they must be framed in the wider scene in which have occurred, related to physical mathematical causes (the work of the Jet Stream) that have determined the weather scenario. If then, even, the statistical

---

1. Mario PINNA, *Climatology*, Chap. 4, Par. 2.

averages are built on "wrong" data the problem becomes a serious error.

The common error in climate research today, as recent past, is not only the way to use the values of the thermal average for the purposes of research, but even in the blind confidence in analysis of specific statistic data. In fact, the values used to compose statistics could not guarantee an and meticulous active control, which is essential to prove the reliability of the source and then working to scientific research on the basis of numbers that are not tainted by obsolete or not up to standard stations.

5.4. Reality behind the statistics: the Jet Stream never lies

Meteo Mundi (Madrigali Theory) has immediately identified the critical importance of an efficient network for statistical detection. To assess the reliability of the data we need to link the atmospheric progressive event (meteorology) with the cause corresponding to the action (Jet Stream of free atmosphere). The reference statistical value must be compared with the complete set of documentation and accurate weather data to the ground (temperature, humidity, pressure, winds, and atmospheric conditions) and the physic–mathematic matrix of their trigger in altitude.

In fact, the physic of the atmosphere (Jet Stream) connected to the lunar force, which shall decide the movements of the arctic or sub–tropical masses of air, triggering the phenomenology on the floor, which can be temporary or constant, as with intervals of persistence and extremism.

The detailed analysis of these data, observed in time and space, reveals unequivocally that the Jet Stream in the free atmosphere has the power to move the thermal energy excess and defect: interfering on air masses, even extreme, hot and cold, and consequently varying considerably the climatic conditions of each corner of the Planet.

The close connection between the specific arrangement of tropospheric flow and the resulting climatic effects detected on the ground is shown with clear evidence making the reconnaissance back in time. Using the *ad hoc* software is in fact possible to reconstruct the progressions of the Jet Stream from past to present, at least in the last two hundred years. Superimposing this diachronic and constant evolution to weather occurrences historically recorded in this or that part of the Earth, there is no doubts on the indissoluble cause–effect relationship between a given configuration of the flow at high altitude and the contemporary's climatic phenomena in the ground.

The whole process triggered by the Jet Stream action concatenated to the lunar force and the her physic–mathematical aspect causes a targeted thermal effect and atmospheric rainfall detected on the ground by meteorological station which gives sensitive effects, identifying the essential parameters such as pressure, temperature and precipitation. Statistic data, detected in corresponding station, is a temperature value intimately tied to the air mass of in motion on the day of the observation, linked to persistence and identification of the baric field in altitudes (Jet Stream).

The proponents of the Global Warming Theory admit that studies are based on numbers provided by a not up to standard or obsolete network of detection. The reference to the Jet Stream action can be a valuable tool to unmask not credible data, deleting them from the calculation, to identify accurately any corrupted stations to replace them or move them to places that are not subject to contamination.

Physic–mathematical data on the incoming air mass, connected to the baric action of tropospheric flow removes any doubt about the reliability of the detection. The meteorological result, as a picture, identifies the complete appearance of the phenomenon detected, by providing an important proof on the veracity of values recorded from the station.

For example, imagine a control unit in the north of Italy, which, in the middle of winter, signals a temperature of 20 degrees centigrade. To verify station reliability the scientists have to superimpose the weather situation in that area at the time of survey, on the number obtained. If there were, in that moment, the presence of a cold component in altitude, the temperature value would clearly not credible and wrong. It would in other words, a photomontage able to disguising reality.

5.5. Misleading data; precipitate conclusions

The exact interpretation of meteorological and statistic data is very important. It allows us to highlight in an unambiguous manner the gravitational–physic–mathematic nature of weather each in the ground, avoiding jumping to quick conclusions about abnormal or atypical temperature increases or decreases in the latitude of reference.

Alleged abnormal changes may be had been breached (in case of incorrect measurements). They are often mistakenly such considered because confirmed by comparison with too short periods (the thirty years 1960–1990); and they are attributed to hypothetical triggering factors (for example anthropic pollution), ignoring the intimate and never interrupted relation with the "natural" evolution of the Jet Stream in the free atmosphere.

A large number of climatologists do not consider the sources of meteorological data, deeming them irrelevant or valid for a short time forecasting. It is precisely this popular idea of "separation" and mutual non–influence between climatology and meteorology that is creating great confusion in the field and conclusions at least debatable in the context of the changing global climate.

The Jet Stream has the task of moving the air masses present on the Planet, from every corner of the atmosphere, triggering with their transit on specific geographical latitudes, certain climate consequences. Each individual atmospheric event on the ground can be explained by studying physic of the atmosphere, following the action of a single air mass emphasized in the latitude by the Jet Stream. The meticulous observation, over the years, has shown that every physical mathematical variation of the tropospheric flow triggers certain and precise weather developments. Thermal meteoric effects are often opposed to the logical evolution of zonal jet.

Chapter VI

Yes, the World cools down

From the poles to the equator clear symptoms

The jet, which is part of dominant motion of the great general circulation of the atmosphere, moves from west to east. In theory, this movement should be constant and straight. In reality, for some of the reasons discussed above, it has a wave movement to (similar to natural curves of a river) and in extreme situations may reverse its gear. If the jet speed in altitude is greater, its procession will be more regular (straight line): this configuration, called high zonal index, is the one in which the global climate evolution is "stable" and less subject to sudden and violent oscillations. An abrupt "descent" or "rising" of a wave of t Jet Stream, with its load of warm or cold air masses, from ideal direction causes instead incisive climatic variations in the areas reached by the jet.

Is imperative identify the Jet Stream configuration, because it causes a whole series of variables that act from altitudes to the ground: these variables are, together with persistence and cyclicity factors, even originated sudden and striking oscillations in the distribution of the heat at different latitudes.

6.1. A heart of ice beats on the poles

Let's look at the whole system of the great general circulation of the atmosphere, starting from the subdivision in independent cells of Jet Stream. First, the high latitudes movement related to the Hadley cell thai is between $60°$ and $90°$ parallels.

A weak atmospheric circulation with current rising on the $60°$ parallel descending on the poles. It forms a field of high pressure to the ground for the presence of very cold air,because it is heavier, but at the same time a field of low pressure at altitude, identified with the name of Polar Vortex, also known by who simply follows the weather forecast on TV.

Polar Vortex is a not sure area that is firmly on the Arctic and Antarctic. It is defined as "semi–permanent" for its constant movement, that we could compare to heart contractions, that allows it to expand or retract in latitude. Its "pulsing" affects the air masses movements and the position of polar front, the line of confluence of the subtropical air masses with polar areas.

The polar front are associated with the flow and Atlantic western classical disturbance that affects thermal processes and meteoric latitudes involved in the process.

The Great general circulation of atmosphere is not only represented by western flow, but is made up of several other variants linked to the arrangement of Jet Stream at different latitudes. These motion's variations, that may be sporadic or frequent, are able to turn, at any time depending on their specific provision, all thermal–meteoric balance in every corner of the Planet.

6.2. A beat: the memorable snowfall in Rome

Strong expansions of Polar Vortex, with their effect on the arrangement of the Jet Stream, were the first cause of some of the most dramatic (and cyclic) collapse of temperature that, in Italy, we remember. For example in 1985, ten centimeters of snow fell in Naples, on December of 1996 when a whole country was in the grip of Siberian frost, or especially on February of 1956, when the Padana plain records for several days at 15 degrees below zero and Rome was struck by a snowfall so memorable as to give rise to two songs. One of which (*The Snow of '56* by Mia Martini) was submitted and rewarded the Sanremo's Festival in 1990, thirty–four years later! In these cases, it was precisely a pulsation of the vortex to triggering the retrograde movement of Jet Stream, in virtue of which the arctic air masses (freezing) instead to go to Russia, China and Japan, went down to visit the South of Europe and Italy in particular.

The second movement is identified by Ferrell's the cell of middle latitudes, where it lays down the column of rising air present on the 60° parallel and descending on the branchdry, arid around the 30° parallel (subtropical zone). To this cell are associated classical evolutions of Oceanic disturbance, with the oscillation of the polar front depending on the pressure exerted by Polar Vortex (expansion or contraction).

The third atmospheric circulation or subtropical Hadley's cell distinguishes the hot zone on the Planet. At the Equator, the confluence of trade winds (north eastern and southeastern constant winds) forces the equatorial branch of the Jet Stream to rise, due to the very hot air lifting with branch descending stabilizer on the 30° parallel. In practice, it creates a rift in tropospheric flow, pointing downwards, presses and creates a stable high–pressure area: the hot air does not salt, the clouds do not form, ii is not raining. The hot Hadley movement explains why this specific latitude extends the most arid areas of the Earth.

The situation is different on the virtual line of the Equator, hinge heat point, placed on the central hemispherical part. At this point, the strong heating from below — due to the great incoming solar energy — and the convergence of trade winds create a point of confluence that exalts strong convective motions and precipitations (hot and humid climate).

6.3. Signals from the tropics

The trade winds, constant winds that are blowing from the northeast to the northern hemisphere and from the southeast to the southern hemisphere, tend to generate the development of the intertropical convergence zone (Itcz). The line of tropical convergence that has normal fluctuations of latitude, between summer and winter, triggered by seasonal change and the astronomical intensity of the Sun, is susceptible to fluctuations also linked to the expansion process and contraction of the polar Vortex.

In recent years, it is experiencing an atypical variation of these fluctuations, and there was found a blatant fault of the Itcz in an extreme variability process, often in contraction compared to periods preceding summer. So, we have disturbed summers.

6.4. Another beat: 2003, hell in Europe

The seasonal trend, that triggers the process of the alternation of half–warm to cold, distinguishes itself for the natural expansion of subtropical band, encouraged by the increased solar radiation boreal of summer and by the contraction of the polar Vortex.

In atypical summer seasons, for example in the new millennium, the euro–mediterranean area has witnessed an very variable action of the Itcz, which undergoes expansions or contractions emphasized by greater or lesser encroachment of tropospheric flow. In certain years, a more southern presence has been found, with the significant withdrawal of the subtropical band more to the south of the standard, as well as a its most northern insistence. The most striking case of radicalization, in this time expanding, is that of the summer of 2003, with its heat wave records that overthrows half of Europe causing dozens of deaths: a really singular phenomenon, as the fanciful definitions attributed to that period attest: "mortal hell", "the hottest summer"…

By observing the movements of the Itcz have emerged well overt signals of the importance of constant pressure toward the South of the Polar Vortex, as well as on its withdrawal from South to North: in particular on certain years, subtropical pressure expansions or contractions are directly related to the movement of the Polar Vortex. The Jet Stream in the free atmosphere inhibits or emphasizes the Hadley's cell that is crucial in the process of dominant effect both toward the warm that toward cold.

The increasingly frequent anomalies can occur in any season of the year, affecting summer and winter in the equinoctial intermediate quarters. A careful and constant observation identifies the precise effects of climate tropospheric flow, in contraction or intrusiveness higher than normal, over vast areas of the Globe. The climate change that it follows accompanied also by striking variation of the Itcz, noticeable in cycles of atypical years, for example the month of July 2011 in which Italy and the most of central Europe had lower down temperature average. We could do various similar examples of periods marked by below or over the average temperatures generated by a precise arrangement of tropospheric flow.

6.5. The new advance of the pack

In Antarctic, a net glacial process of expansion is active since several years. The Arctic is in the initial phase of recovery of the pack: only on winter of 2012, he touched again thirty years average in winter, but there are important events that confirm the trend. Among these, one particularly resounding, which the explorer Divide Peluzzi will explain later is the increase of icy surfaces on the east coast of Greenland with an extension of the pack and union with Iceland, which took place on December 22, 2011.

In short, both poles are having a cooling process. The fact that it is manifesting before and with greater virulence in the one part rather than on the other has two fundamental explanations. The first one is the climate difference which is to have between one hemisphere and the other for the presence of a different extension of continental surface, that is more extend on the northern hemisphere than on the Southern hemisphere.

Then there is the question of the underwater volcanic activity. The recent observation of the Arctic revels a progressive increase of the extension sea ice in winter, however, it offsets by a conspicuous reduction summer. This "compensation" does not involve hypothetical processes of anthropic heating of the Planet. The cause only is the presence of a mighty underground geothermal action on the seabed of the Arctic, discovered due to a strong volcanic activity in recent times. Deepening research and submarine surveys have shown that in the Arctic Ocean is to the work a large number of volcanoes, with hydrothermal activity much more powerful than scientists had suspected.

From the depths of the North Pole is raised the ridge Gakkel, a gigantic submarine volcanic mountain that it extends range for 1125 miles from Greenland to Iceland and to Siberia, passing the Arctic, with a width of 125 miles and summits that rise up to 625 miles from the sea surface. For its vigorous "liveliness" causes a geothermal effect that produces considerable effects on the pack extension. They will be studied and monitored.

An important surprise to this recent discovery, it was the unexpected presence under the Arctic of active volcanic energy (craters of 2 km) with a geothermal effect amplified by many hydrothermal springs.

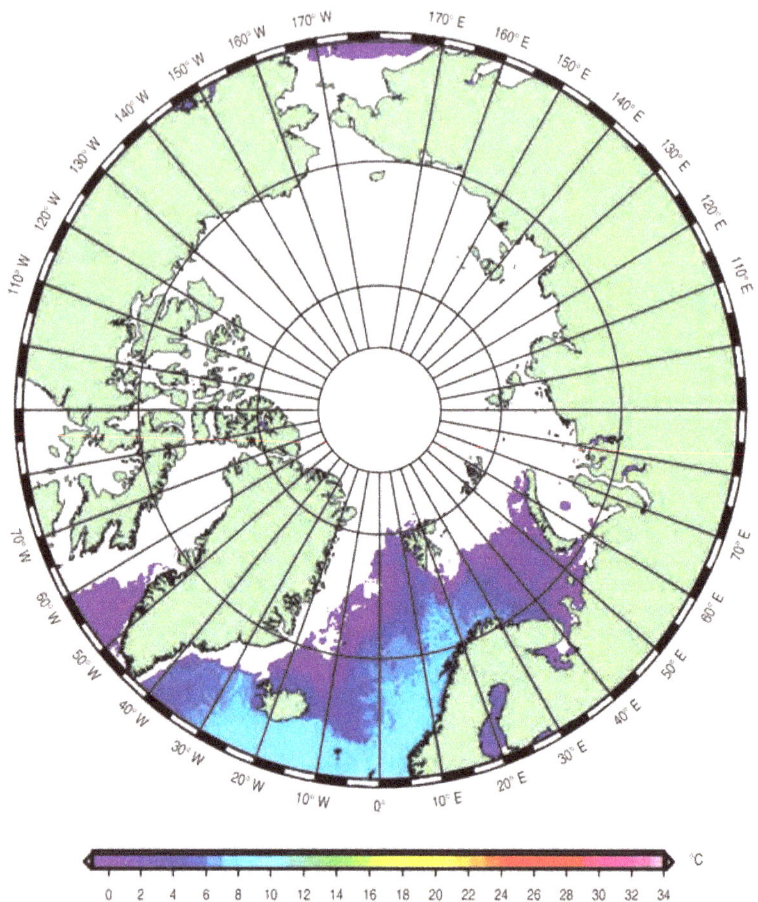

Figure 6.1. DMI

An exceptional discovery that opens up new horizons and concrete answers, about the extension variation of the Arctic pack in recent decades, that was affected and has always suffered in the past this mighty geothermal heating action. Certainly, it is a further proof of the groundlessness of the cause–effect of pack reduction, attributed to the anthropic GW and the confirmation that is the trigger to promote the great difference in process of pack extension between the two ice caps, the Antarctic increasing and the Arctic in deficit on summer.

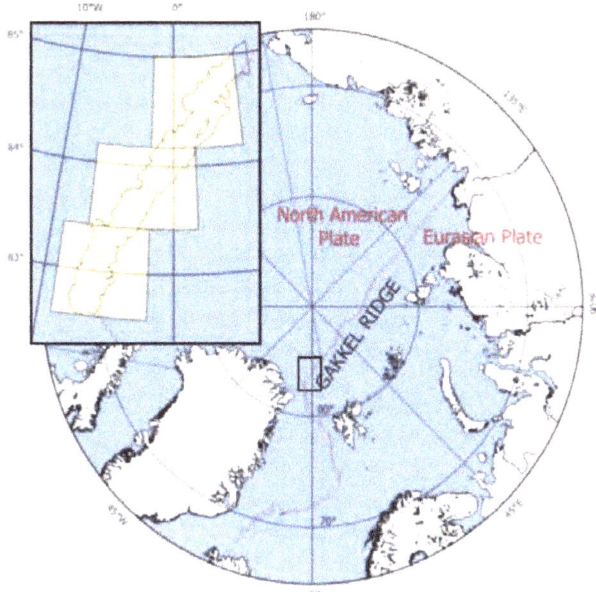

Figure 6.2. Alfred Wegener Institute.

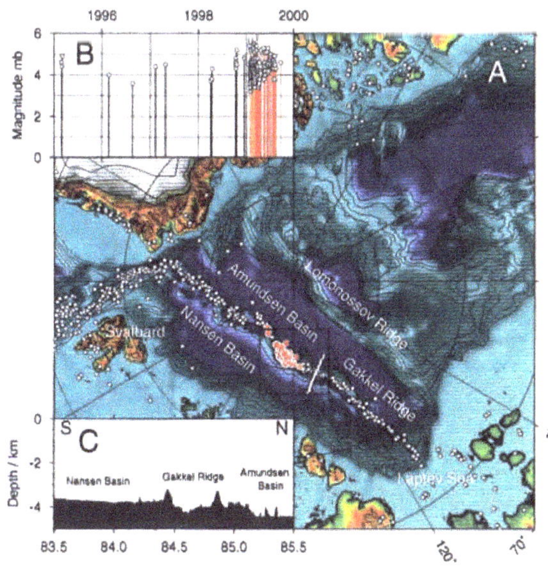

Figure 6.3. Graph of earthquake swarm accompanied by volcanic eruption (Alfred Wegener Institute).

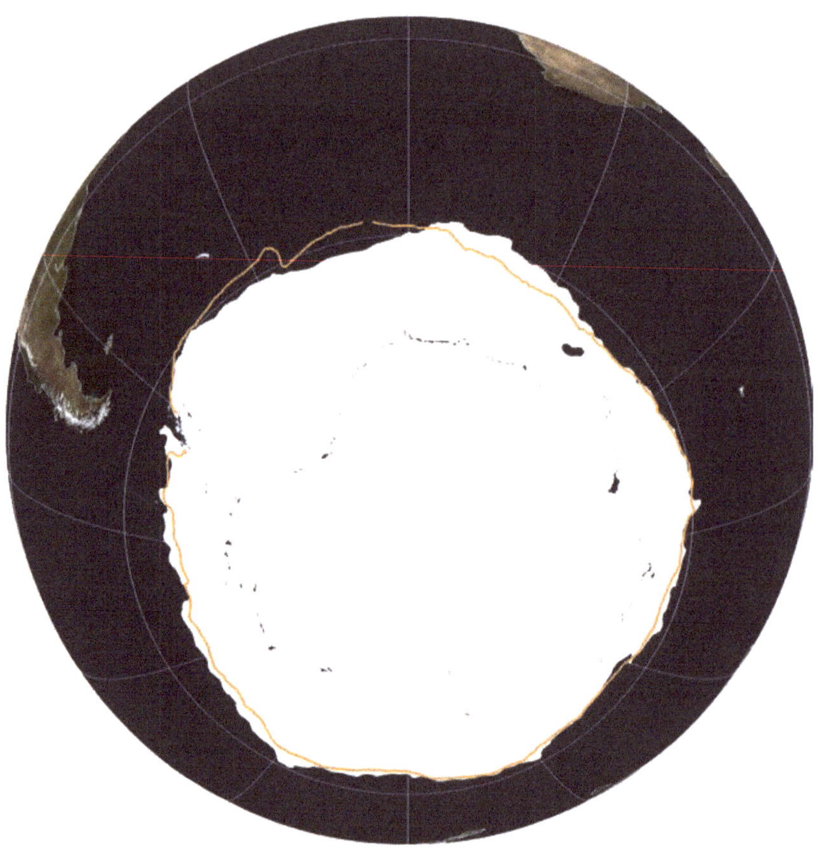

Figure 6.4. Extension of the Antarctic pack that is revealing a strong expansion process.

Chapter VII

In summary

Collect our luggage before to take of the Moon

In summary, we return to the heart of the Madrigali Theory, the analysis of the great general circulation of the atmosphere.

7.1. The big machine determines the climate

The great circulation has a decisive incidence on climate of the entire Planet, exercised through the Jet Stream at every latitude and longitude. This influence is modulated by pulsations of polar vortexes, which are genuine cold forges.

The Great movement have to balancing and distributing, in every part of the Planet, the thermal energy (hot and cold) generated by the different impact of the Sun's rays on the spherical surface of the Earth at different latitudes, with the complicating seasonal furthered by the tilt of Earth's axis.

Between the theoretical atmospheric circulation and the real one, there is a big difference about the distribution of surplus energy. If the planet had not rotated on its axis and had leaded the perfect and constant thermal balance on the Planet, the theoretical movement would be as we told above. The Earth turns on itself and it complicates the climate mechanism by introducing into the various forces involved, as the gravity, the centrifugal force, up to the most important Coriolis' law.

The centrifugal force divides the two theoretical mega–cells in various cells, producing the Great general circulation of atmosphere, its functions and its decisive effects on the Earth's climate evolution.

7.2. The fuel is the Sun

For a long time, it was thought that the nearest star (the Sun) caused hot and cold cycles on the Planet, believing that these had linked to the solar cycle and solar spots. In reality, the Sun has the task to providing energy for the weather–climate gear, which in its absence will slowly stop in less than two months.

Some researchers are convinced that the variation of solar activity interferes on climate change. They have assumed that greater or lesser presence of suns pots causes a climate difference (warmer or colder climate). In reality, the correlation between minimum of sunspots and cold period, referred to the SGE (Small Glacial Era 1500 >1870), is not convincing. The results from different parts of the world indicate that it is unlikely that it was a global cooling. A variation of the JS (Jet Stream) and tropospheric circulation, with a heat redistribution among various parts of the planet is more plausible. There is no proofs that cold period involved every part of Europe. Reading the chart taken from an historical research on climate of the scientist Cristian Pfister[1], it should be noted that climatic variations (both toward cold and both toward hot) from 1536 to 1675 are already present before the minimum of Maunder[2]. In addition, we realize, observing the data, they suffer frequent changes during the time respect to linear issuing of solar energy.

7.3. The distributor and the Jet Stream

The climate change on our planet has origin in the atmosphere's dynamics and in particular in the arrangement of the Great general circulation under the influence of polar Vortex. The position assumed by the Jets Stream has a strategic function connected to the manner in which distributes the thermal energy at different latitudes. The

---

1. Christian PFISTER, Professor of Economic, social and environmental history (WSU). Research interest: historical climatology, environmental history, population history, agricultural history (http://www.hist.unibe.ch/content/personal/pfister_christian/index_ger.html#e326).

2. Maunder Minimum: 1645–1715, minimum of sunspots discovered by astronomer Edward Walter MAUNDER (1851–1928).

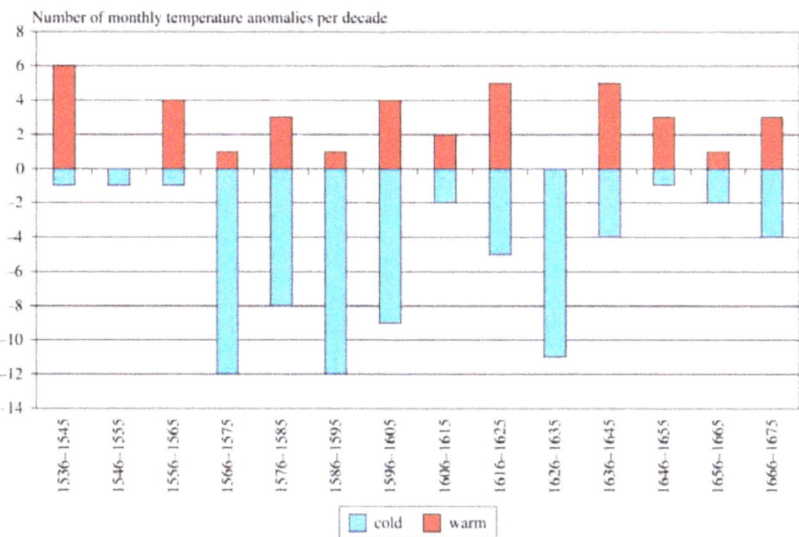

Figure 7.1. Decennial Sum of Extremely Cold and Warm Anomalies During the Summers (April to September) from 1536 to 1675 in Switzerland, North of the Alps (Data basis: Pfister, Raum–zeitliche Rekonstruktion: 106–16).

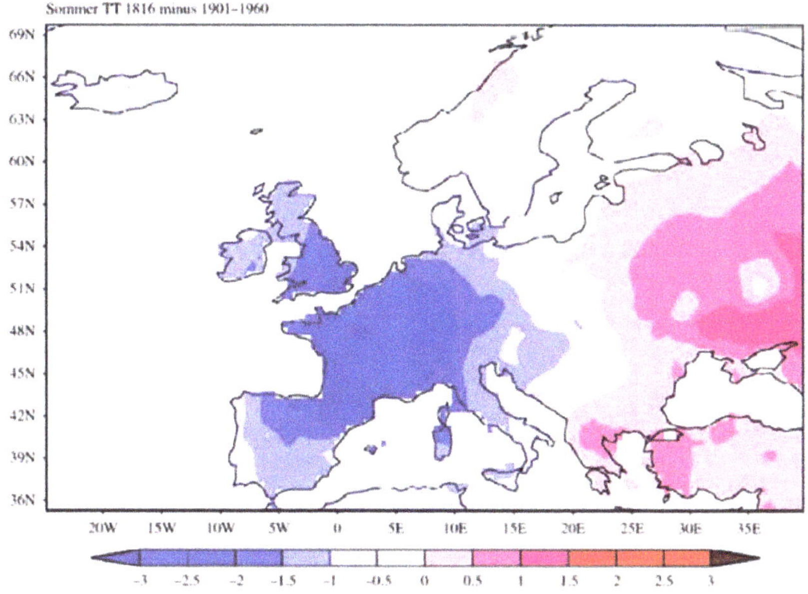

Figure 7.2. Temperature Distribution in Europe in the "Year without Summer" (1816). Deviation of Temperature in Summer 1816 from the 1901–60 Average.

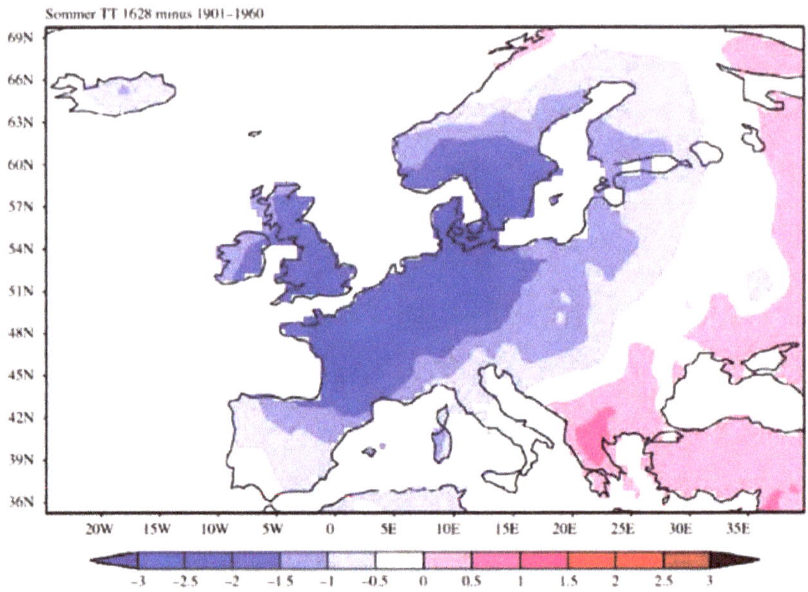

Figure 7.3. Temperature Distribution in Europe in the "Year without Summer" (1816). Deviation of Temperature in Summer 1628 from the 1901–60 Average.

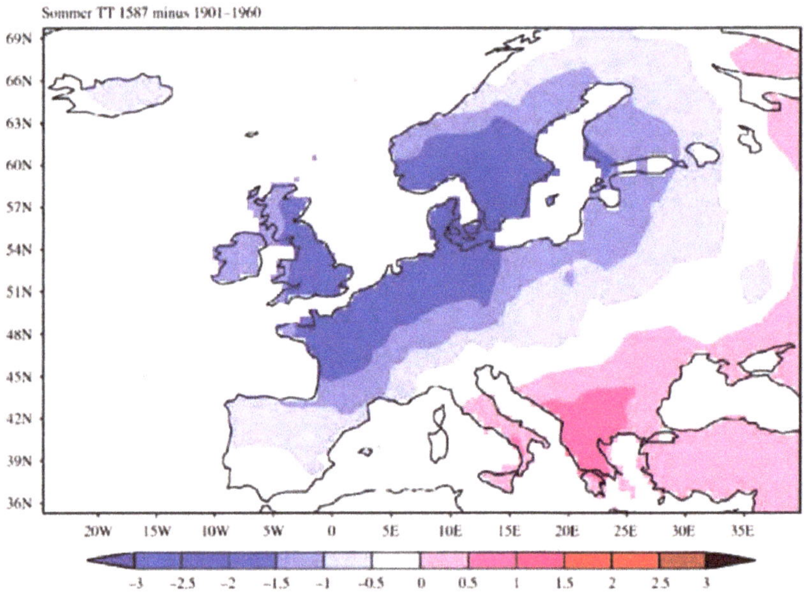

Figure 7.4. Temperature Distribution in Europe in the "Year without Summer" (1816). Deviation of Temperature in Summer 1587 from the 1901–60 Average.

tropospheric flow transports air cold and hot masses (arctic / tropical), and locates them on certain areas, with cyclic cadences, constructing the periodical variations that have forged the past large thermal cycles and that they will beat them in the future.

7.4. Refrigeration effect or boiler effect: air masses

The air masses of are a hinge point of the whole climate system. Different air masses generate, with their transit and thanks to their thermal nature (which is closely linked to the origin region), significant climatic changes also in the same latitude: They can be Arctic or Subtropical but with their meridian zonal and anti–zonal movements, they always affect the weather.

An air mass is born when it is stayed for a long time on a geographical, homogeneous and much–extended environment, either oceanic or continental, nurturing unique characteristics. the names of the most significant air portions generated by the Great general circulation of atmosphere are the "arctic" air, "polar" air and the "subtropical" air, always separated in "maritime" (sea influence) and "continental" (originated on the continents).

7.5. The input of Vortices

The central motor of the General atmospheric circulation are the Polar Vortices. They give control the distribution of the Rossby's waves, their width, length and depth of penetration; and through these the Great circulation directs and displaces, at a global level, the low and high pressure areas, associated with hot and cold air, and with all phenomenology that they are responsible.

The high–pressure centers to the middle latitudes are baric situations associated with atmospheric stability and rising subtropical hot air, which distinguish one period of atmospheric improvement. The low–pressure areas are associated with clouds and precipitation, with very cold polar air, which is dislodging at different latitudes in penetration toward the South, causing thermal and climate differences.

These atmospheric changes generated by the arrangement and movement of high and low pressure centers represent the climate necessity linked to the dynamism and vitality of polar vortices. They are cold vortices, depending on their expansion or contraction, encourage a greater or lesser dominant pejorative atmospheric in the various climatic zones of Earth.

The polar Vortex shrinks in summer, causing a less efficiency and intrusiveness of the Jet Stream to the South exalting the warm season; it expands itself in winter, causing the dominant deterioration in this season.

In neutral period, Polar Vortex produces a "uniform" climatic global distribution. Latitudes feel the effect of their geographical locations and their specific territorial parameters, with regular and well–spelled seasons.

7.6. At the mercy of "crazy hearts"

If we compared the Polar Vortex movement to the heart one, we noted that it is a "crazy heart". The meteorological and thermal context begin complicate for the pulsation in expansion or contraction of the Polar Vortex (typical cyclicity within the climate mechanism) here is that it everything the meteorological and heat. The Vortex toward the South marks a succession of altered seasonal cycles: the alternation of regular weather is replaced by a chaotic and mixed situation in the various months of the year, with extreme phenomena on the ground reducing the "oceanicity". The degenerative tendency intensifies, in particular, the thermal excesses, fed by the lack of regular distribution of thermal energy at different latitudes.

In this context, meteorological events can intensify themselves: the areas subject to pressing or constant precipitation over the average for period, other affected by long periods of drought.

Meteo Mundi Research (Madrigali Theory) records meteorological parameters who build the real terrestrial climate average. The result is obtained by analyzing a vast amount of values detected by a dense weather stations network able to observe the cause–effect of the action of the Great general circulation of atmosphere and the Jet Stream at altitudes and on the ground.

A persistence of climatic events identifies a precise climate cycle or period controlled by Polar Vortex and the Great circulation, which is manifested by the variations registered by weather stations.

In the recent past, it is found that the strong expansion of the polar Vortex (from 1950 to the late seventies), as well as a subsequent period of contraction, persistent in the eighties–ninety of the last century.

7.7. 1950–1975: when you cried cooling anthropogenic

In the five decades between 1950 and 1975 the Earth has experienced a process of expansion of arctic deterioration: Bad turn in the weather, marked by more rigid alternated with tormented summers. From the data on weather observations at reference period, emerge that, inside of those twenty–five years, hot and torrid situations verified, always in a prevailing pejorative context. The warm prefrontal were less frequent due to the intense ripple of polar flow in the summer period and often they had summers similar to autumns for the influence of tropospheric flow during hot the quarter.

In that particular period, however, the winters were more often cold and snowy and the glaciers were raised. The public was convinced, accomplice of the authoritative TV and printed–paper opinion, to be in the presence of a global cooling that would have led in a short time to a new ice age.

Curiously, also in that period they found the responsible of the pollution: the man, they said, is entering into the atmosphere an abnormal amount of dust that favor the aggregation of the droplets (coalescence) and the formation of the clouds, with consequent rains, greater reflection of solar energy and cooling. This theory was also supported by people that, fifteen years later, would begin to evoke the exact opposite, the Global Warming, because we were in a new climate optimum (the period of twenty years Eighty–Ninety) with an increase of climate averages of the Planet. The powders that in the twenty–five years earlier would have had to freeze the world had been replaced by CO_2, that the world would have had to melt as an ice cream.

7.8. Third Millennium, the cold returns

The Great climate machine continues unflappable in his natural path always heedless of both propitiate rites and pseudo–ecologist anathemas.

Between a "inexplicable phenomenon" and a "phenomenal explanation", we believe in facts: a new process in place, started in the Third Millennium and pronounced in 2008, with complicate winters in many areas of the Planet. A trend, to make a tangible example, which is worsening in Italy (in particular in the North, but not only), where, respect to the eighties–ninety of the last century, snowfall increase, in plain as in mountain, in the cold quarter, with same pauses.

The climate observation records an increasingly strong intrusiveness of the flow in altitude. This increased pressure toward the South of the Arctic flow induces a prevalence of arctic cold air, which generates rigid winters and snowy to medium–high latitudes. The forecasting chronology of recent years on the progression of the cold quarter in Europe, Asia and North America reveals a succession of icy and snowy events. An increase process for frequency and intensity, which causes not a few socio–economic problems in the countries concerned by the phenomenon.

7.9. From the Pole to the Tropics, a march led by Jet Stream

Any climate process, be it an improvement or worsening, starts from medium–high latitudes, where the pressure and interference of Arctic and Antarctic depressions are more significant, induced by the process of contraction (optimum) or expansion (cooling).

The first latitudes, that are affected, are those near to the Arctic Circle, with subsequent expansion to the South, a gradual inexorable process. In this sense, the Jet Stream assumes a decisive role, accentuating the pejorative process especially on concrete geographical locations. This process occurs with more emphasis in particular where the tropospheric flow arrangement has already a strong influence.

It is reiterates the importance of climatic effect of the Jet Stream in geographical areas located at the same latitude. The Jet Stream creates a different prevalent climate pressure, triggering strong thermal disparity and rainwater at the same latitude. For example, New York, city of the United States, is located on the 41° parallel as Naples, Italy. In the "Big Apple", snow and frost are frequent, with relevant values: isotherms to 1400/1500 mt that can even exceed −14°. In Naples, instead, the snow on the ground is a rarity, a sort of climate "miracle"; in winter sometimes, we can go out without coat with temperatures above zero. Simple differences of air masses, recalled at altitude by the Jet Stream.

Staying on the 41° parallel, but moving toward the East, we realize that difference can be acute. Thermal disparities with the same latitude are even more glaring, in some cases devastating. Everything is under the action of the Jet Stream.

Other concrete evidence of climatic power of the Jet Stream is the strong thermal difference between Scotland, Canada and Southern Greenland (looking west), and between Scotland and Siberia, looking to the east. A "markedly uneven" climatic band although, all they are around the 56° parallel. Radical differences generated by the manner in which the Jet Stream takes place on each area, exalting continental features or the action of maritime places.

The relative sweetness climate of Scotland with respect to its "sisters of latitude" is not only related to the presence of the Gulf Stream, which mitigates the European coastal climate. To accentuate the difference in temperatures between the British island and, for example, and the Canadian city of Edmonton, once again the Jet Stream, which on Canada conveys icy air masses picked up from the Arctic and transported through extended continental surfaces. On Scotland brings air masses, which, in its movement from west to east, has made to pass on oceanic surfaces. Masses that then, continuing on their journey toward the east, return to cool down while flying over the boundless territories of North Eurasia, until to creating drastic frost in Moscow and in Siberia.

The Gulf Stream[3] is a permanent phenomenon. Therefore, if it were the only responsible of the relative mildness of Scotland, we would have a stable climatic situation and free of excess heat. In reality, however, also the latitudes of the north–center of Europe, wetted by

---

3. Gulf Stream: hot ocean current that comes from the Gulf of Mexico and which mitigates the climate of European countries bordering the Atlantic Ocean.

the generous "hot" marine current, often suffer the effects of an arctic active pressure, which generates extreme cold and heavy snowfall.

It is the Jet Stream, with its persistence baric configuration with cyclic variables cadences of the half–waves of the tropospheric flow that induces everywhere on the Planet, climatic and sensitive variations. This is the "supreme power" of the Great General circulation of atmosphere, hat only arranging the Jet Stream and diversifying its movement in time and space triggers thermal intense marked situations. Earth's climate is not randomly distributed and it should be according to the latitude, but is bound to the action of the Jet Stream. This force positions and builds high and low pressure centers, enhancing specific climate effects where the continental surface is more extended.

7.10. A simple pirouette overturns the World

To have a clearer idea of the role of the Jet Stream (and of the great movement) in the determination of the global climate can we build an imaginary scenario, for example. As we have already noted, in a theoretical framework "ideal" temperature differences from one part to another of the terrestrial sphere would be linked exclusively to the greater or lesser amounts of daily / annual exposure to the heat of the Sun's rays and to the inclination of the same rays (more or less oblique or direct). In fact, it is not just for the presence and action of the great movement, which is connected to the orbital motions of the Earth, the Sun and the Moon. Among the phenomena that "complicate" further this general framework there is, and we have seen, the rotation of the Earth on itself. This constant rotation is defined by counterclockwise convention and it follows the prevalent movement from the west to the east of the Great general circulation, and therefore the Jet Stream.

Now, let us try to imagine that suddenly, the Earth reversed the direction of travel of its rotation on itself, from clockwise to time. Even the Jet Stream, at that point, spill onto its course, taking to travel from east to west. This simple "U turn" would change radically the face of the planet, by overturning the scenario global climate to which we are accustomed to and in which the life — including the human civilization — has developed over millions of years.

Moving from east to west, in fact, the Jet Stream would lead the masses of arctic frosty air toward Europe, without pass on Atlantic Ocean surfaces and transiting on the huge "cooling" northern Euro–Asian continental surfaces. On the Mediterranean, therefore, we would constantly have freezing air: penguins would populate the Faraglioni of Capri while the Sun of Long Island would products limoncello[4].

4. Limoncello: typical digestive alcoholic lemon drink produced in the South of Italy.

Chapter VIII

The return of the Ice Age

Chronicle of an announced problem

8.1. Bad news from the Polar Circles

The "great" situation that has just been outlined can be useful also to better understand the very real phenomenon, crucial and in some ways tragic, to which we mentioned earlier: the cooling process in place at the poles.

From the Arctic and Antarctic, we have seen that with the opening of the new millennium the temperatures have resumed sharply to decrease. This process of thermal decrease, which binds to the expansion of the pack, is faster and more evident in the Southern hemisphere, while in the Northern Hemisphere where it seems evident only in the last few years.

Both the cooling process in progress that the disagreement time with which this process occurs in the two poles have a scientific explanation, bonded to the Great general circulation action of atmosphere (originated by Polar Vortices expansive movement) and the specific "geography" of the hemispheres.

8.2. Thermal inertia and geothermal energy: Arctic late–onset, the Antarctic runs fast

On the Northern hemisphere the presence of a much broader continental extension (emerged lands) tends to delay the process, by virtue of the thermal inertia, and of an albedo effect more virulent. Plains and reliefs promote the deposition of snow and the formation of glaciers and at the same time emphasize input climate induced by tropospheric flow. Everything (more or less, than what is usual when it speaks of "continental climate") produces marked thermal inversions, which are to generate especially on the Asian continent north, but also (with strong increases in temperature) on continents to tropical–equatorial latitudes. The extremes, in some way, they are balance yet.

We say "yet", because the situation suddenly and quickly may degenerate (toward cooling). This happens especially when on the arctic hemisphere will run out the effects of the thermal inertia.

The continental surfaces tend to accumulate greater amounts of cold and heat. They absorb more, and spend more time to release that they have absorbed. A phenomenon of which we all always concrete experience: the maximum solar heating takes place in the month of June, when the rays pointing straight to the ground; but the warm is percived on ground two months later, in August, when the action of the Sun joins the heat gradually released from the continent. the same happen during the winter, when the minimum irradiation occurs in December, but the "big chill" comes between January and February, "the blackbird's days"[1] as in Italy we define this period.

The hemisphere arctic therefore, with its overt continental areas, in this moment is still releasing what remains of the heat absorbed in twenty "hot" years between the Eighties and Nineties of the last century. This fact, combined with the presence of strong submarine geothermal activity of which we have already said, limits the perception of the effects of the general cooling in act.

On the contrary, the southern hemisphere, oceanic, has already begun his inevitable "race to the cold". The reference period 2000–2013 has in fact shown, in comparison with the Eighties–Ninety, a sharper and more consistent extension of the ice pack of the South Pole.

On the North Pole instead, the effect of thermal inertia, derived from the climate optimum in the last two decades of the Twentieth

---

1. The blackbird's days are, according to tradition, the last three days of January (29, 30 and 31). Also according to tradition would be the three coldest days of the year (although some legends and traditions as they specify variant the last two days of January and February 1st). According to other sources the term derives from a legend in which, sheltering from the extreme cold, a blackbird and her chicks, originally white, took refuge inside a chimney, they emerged from it on February 1st and they were blacks for the soot. From that day all blackbirds are blacks.

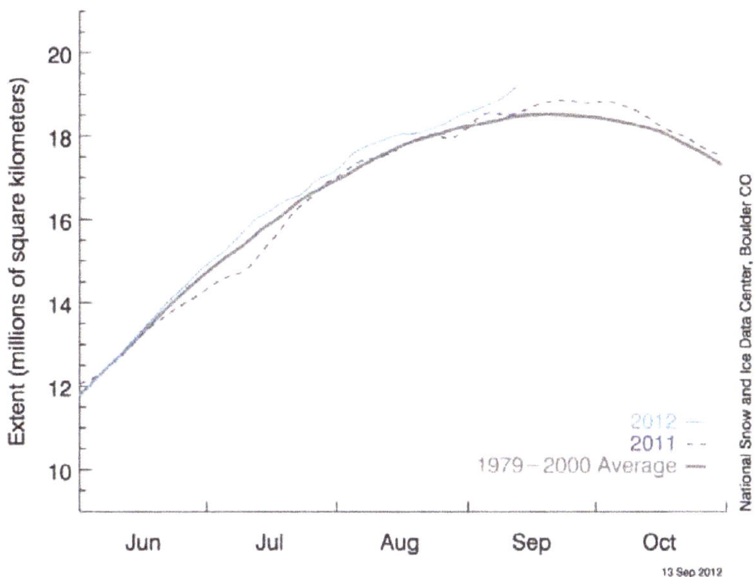

Figure 8.1. Antarctic Sea Ice Extent (area of ocean with at least 15% sea ice).

Century, is prolonged, recording the maximum contraction of the arctic pack in 2007. A process of long wave and suffering of the arctic pack also extended from geological vivacity underlying it.

Today, and in particular from 2009, it is highlighting the initiation of a slow process in reverse, with a new gradual enlargement of the icy winter surface. An evolution confirmed by reaching, after years of reduction, of the thirty years reference average with regard to the extension of the Arctic ice cover in the winter season 2011–12.

8.3. Time's up: the global frost is on the prowl

The prospect more disturbing: when the Arctic Vortex in expansion, exhausted the thermal inertia effect, will product similar effects to those generated by the Antarctic Vortex, the weather–climate situation will exponentially degenerate. At that precise point in time there will be a process of lowering world thermal increasingly acclaimed, that

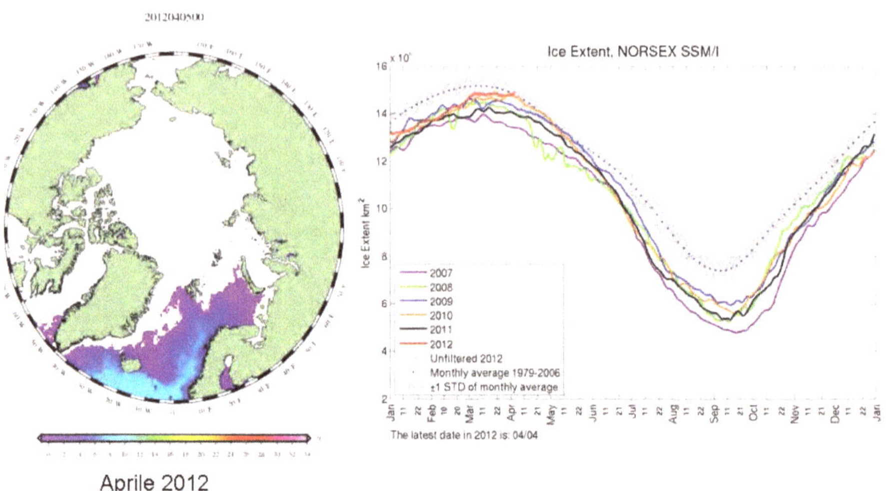

Figure 8.2. Ice Extent, DMI.

will drag inexorably the Earth toward the passage thermal historically inevitable: the next ice age.

The past as a metronome and the present as a symptom announce the news that scholars more attentive and free of prejudices expect: the next thermal step of the Planet will be a strong cooling process followed by the arrival of the new ice age. A global intense process, which is repeated, as regulated by a Swiss watch every 11.000–11.500 years.

The time at our disposal is practically concluded: the climate pendulum, which always swings alternating long glacial eras to "brief" interglacial era, has reached a peak and now it is preparing to precipitate toward the opposite peak.

The interglacial era in which we live and that has allowed to the human civilization growing and developing in optimal conditions, is finished, the limit of the fatidic 11,500 years of life. In the near future, therefore, the Earth can only promise a glaciation. The same phenomenon that probably extinct the race of dinosaurs and that, cyclically, it was able to clear in a single blow up to 75 per cent of the species living on the planet, without giving them time and way to defend themselves.

8.4. The point of no return: any time is good

From now on, every moment could be that good. An issue to bear in mind, it will not be a slow and gradual process. A medium–short period of cooling that seems starting from this Millennium; it might be sufficient to trigger the "point of no return": an unstoppable and exponential acceleration to the ice age and its one hundred thousand years (on average) of persistence. This means that for one hundred thousand years Earth will offer favorable conditions for the human race survival, according to the current parameters and the current technological knowledge, only in a very small portion of its surface, which extends more or less between the equator and tropics.

The Jet Stream will transmit the march of the great cold, once again, with a colder air masses continuity to deploy on the entire planet.

8.5. Follow the Jet Stream to forestall

For these reasons a constant and effective monitoring of the meteorological degeneration process in act, which can be seen analyzing the moves of tropospheric flow at different latitudes, seems essential, today. We need not only thermal medium but also a climate statistic built on meteorological data collected in across the time, to locate changing of climate pressure at different latitudes.

The study of the tropospheric flow has highlighted the crucial importance not only to climate change at altitudes, but also in the oscillations in global expansion (cooling) or to contraction (heating).

We have noted the role played by the distribution and the geographical extension of continental areas, and the cause–effect of Jet Stream in the thermal variations on various Planet's areas placed at the same latitude.

We noted, as during every heating or cooling process to the ground a simultaneous, specific pressure and diversification of the Jet Stream at altitude. The different configurations at altitude have a direct impact on the ground, amplified at certain latitudes and influenced by geographical locations and by microclimates.

This scenario is a fundamental "revelation" because it shows how the tropospheric flow, in addition to trigger individual climate change, also directs the evolution of process, in the direction of the global warming or cooling. Following it and interpreting it, we may predict important and long–term "climate trends".

Take for example everything that happened in the last twenty years of the last century, it has "unleashed" the suggestion of global warming. If, in the late seventies, we had analyzed (as today the Madrigali Theory makes) movements of the entire air column of, from the ground to altitude, we could have easily observed as the component in altitude, in that period, had slowed its activities. A sort of persistent stalemate in which the cold air masses were relegated in northern areas of the Globe. Knowing that dynamic, we would have been able to predict the global climate trend of following the twenty years: it is "hot", but not for the action of the anthropogenic pollution but for the stabilizing effects linked to momentary stage of Jet Stream "quiet".

8.6. The parallels, key sensors

The key that allows you to recognize the path begun by Jet Stream (toward the warming or toward the cooling) was precisely this observation of what happens, from a climate point of view, at the same time in different geographical areas of the World arranged on the same parallel. These locations become the real sensors, able to detecting and detect the occurrence of an inevitable thermal process.

In fact, as we have highlighted, explaining, for example, the strong differences of climate averages between New York and Naples or between the North of Canada and Scotland, the tropospheric flow, with its air masses, influences more some areas than others. Jet Stream is more "intrusive" in some areas; its specific configuration (hot or cold) affects the ground in a direct and extreme manner. In winter of 2012–2013 may also happen that in Naples there was no temperature decrease ; while in New York, on February 2013 unleashed "the storm of the century", with record snowfalls and Siberian temperatures. The same happened, proceeding toward the east on the same "Line", in Japan, China and Korea that, compared to this line is more Southern.

That is happening in New York (or in East), gives us the measure of the force of tropospheric flow and provides the diagnosis about his state of health. Then, if this diagnosis is confirmed by multiannual persistence, the global trend becomes explicit.

8.7. New frontiers for the weather forecast

The study on the Jet Stream and on the great general circulation of the atmosphere opens new frontiers to the accuracy of short medium and long term weather forecasts. Borders that could prove extremely valuable: just think how could be worth, in economic terms, the preventive awareness to be entered into a long cold period. Whole nations could equip themselves for their social and productive organization to the changed climatic conditions. They may be planning appropriate strategies to supply energies or to save energy, or changing the mobility and infrastructure system to avoid tragedies such as those happened, between 2012 and 2013, on the Russia's motorways paralyzed by frost.

Raising the alert level is necessary now. In fact, we are witnessing to a process of global cooling where the outcome is not obvious. It could be concluded in twenty years (as between 1956 and 1975), followed by a new period of optimum. Indeed, if we were at the beginning or in the middle of an interglacial era, this return path to hot would be almost obvious. Since the interglacial era is ending, a cooling period is much more worrying than a heating cycle, as a potential cause of the famous "point of no return" to the glaciation.

The transition from the current interglacial stage to the new ice age will begin with repetition of tortious action on warmer seasons (spring and summer). A constant nuisance, through the Jet Stream, would cause a devastating cause–domino effect, laying the foundations for a process of transition to the next glaciation, now imminent (in the coming decades). The final passage to the new ice age will not be linear and constant, but will produces a series of cause–effect. This will happen with varied and stormy baric dispositions that will determine a process of climate change in which the extreme will be a rule. This rule can progressively diminish at the end of the process with the dominance of a new dominant polar cold, which will be the reference for the new ice age.

The purpose of the research carried out by Madrigali Theory — Meteo Mundi is to have calculation tools with realize increasingly reliable even in long range forecasting, able to prevent the arrival of important and persistent thermal variations, it means cooling or warming cycles.

Chapter IX

Earth's future is written in the Moon

Our small satellite can change the destiny of the World

9.1. The Jet Stream regulates the climate. Who does regulate the Jet Stream?

We have highlighted how strategically monitoring the Jet Stream movements is important for a correct interpretation of climate change that have succeeded during millions of years, but also for more accurate short term forecasts of climate trends. A necessary approach to understand "what happened" and "what happens", but it is still insufficient to fully understand 'what will happen". Monitoring, "follows" the Jet Stream's moves, but cannot anticipate them.

The decisive and revolutionary step is identify the first reason that induces, in time and space the different moves of the Jet Stream. Knowing in advance how, where and when it will act, will give us a never even imagined knowledge: the knowledge of future climate change, the ability to predict accurately, punctually and scientifically the weather for years.

9.2. The strength of the Moon: an important discovery

The "reason" he finally has "a body and a name". The answer to one of the most profound mysteries of always, the evolution of the climate, hovering on the head of humanity from time immemorial, but none so far had collection although there were very clear signals. One in all, the cyclicality constant variations in the flow with a rate of two–four weeks: exactly the times of the phases of the Moon. It is precisely the Moon, with its gravitational force, the keystone of the entire process. It is the Moon to give input to configurative moves the Jet Stream and therefore to the evolutions planetary climate. It is the Moon the instrument, and now we are going to prove it, that may allow forecasts accurate weather and very long range.

The future is already written in the Moon. This is the sensational "discovery" to which the multiannual research of Madrigali Theory have produced.

9.3. From Intuition to certainties

The astronomical observatory of Grosseto, in the hamlet of Roselle in this discovery, has played an essential role. A place with an exceptional beauty landscape overlooking the Tuscan hills, in an area of high archeological Etruscan and Roman interest.

The observatory of Grosseto is the second most important astronomical pole of Tuscany and participates in prestigious national and international research projects, among which the Issp (ASV Supernova Research Project). At Roselle, the insights on the influence of gravitational motions in the "great game" of the evolving global climate have found solid confirmations, also thanks to the valuable scientific physical and astronomical advice provided the Madrigali Theory, by numerous and accredited staff.

The Madrigali Theory has studied in depth the dynamics of the Great general circulation of atmosphere, understanding and to certifying the role of "single engine" on climate. This point is not enough. The research team has always pointed to the following step: find the missing piece, the last ring of the chain in the gear of perfect climate machine. In fact, if the tropospheric flow determines every climate phenomenon to the ground with its changes in speed, direction, and persistence, we will have to find the cause that determines those variations in flow.

9.4. Issue of cycles

The variations of the tropospheric flow are cyclic, in two / four weeks it modulates the speed (from maximum to minimum) and the prevalent direction.

To explain this variability of movement of Jet Stream someone has used the action of the friction force on the continents: slowing down or displacements, linked to the passage of the current in areas of specific geographical connotations. This theory is not persuasive. Primarily, because the stream flows at a very distance from Earth, between 5 and 12 kilometers in height, and is not easy imagine a "contact" with the ground. Above all because, even if this contact existed, the cyclicality of changes in time would remain inexplicable.

Therefore, there should exist a "higher power" that acts directly on the flow and produces these important changes, forcing it to speed and direction important changings.

In the research, we have understand the need to turn gaze to astronomical forces where finding an answer. In the observatory of Grosseto began an intense scientific work about a possible relationship between the vector gravitational forces in game in the "triangulation" Earth–Moon–Sun and the changes in the tropospheric flow.

The results arrived quickly. Comparison by comparison, the gravitational formulae revealed a perfect coincidence with the physical mathematical climate change models, confirming the original insight: there is a direct r cause–effect relationship between the evolutions of Jet Stream and the closest to us satellite: the Moon.

9.5. Maree, proverbs, legends, Kepler and Newton: the future is not a surprise

Is it an amazing truth? No it is not, if we thinking about an interesting natural phenomenon that is explained scientifically and clarified, certified by centuries: the tides, and generally the displacement of large liquid masses above and below the planet surface, certain specifically caused by the Moon's "spins".

The Moon and is a key factor in the specific "liveliness" of Earth, and his protagonist role is clear, with full evidence, compared to other planets of the solar system without satellite. For example, Mars that — losing his satellite — it is transformed into an inert mass, without volcanic activity, atmosphere and without atmospheric phenomenology.

Certainly the equation "phases of the Moon = climate change" is not a new for a peasant of other times, which attributed to certain configurations of the satellite, following a logic carved in dozens and dozens of similar proverbs in every corner of the World,very precise consequences for the weather. We know that culture has always connected the lunar movements to the concept of "change". Overflying fantastic aspects (lycanthropy) or pseudo–psychological definitions (who changes easily mood is "lunatic"), it is curious that men always has the connected Moon's phases to biological transformation, parallel to the evolution, declining or increasing, of the night satellite : from wine in the barrels to hair, from nails to agriculture. In all instable elements, we note the influence of the Moon.

This is not science but suggestion, from which we have to keep away. Certainly, the large part of sayings and mottos have left unfounded beliefs, but behind this, there is the millenary and prescientific intuition, of an "intimate" relationship between the Earth dynamism and dance around its satellite that deserves not to be ignored.

The path taken by Madrigali Theory and team of Meteo Mundi has nothing to do with myths and legends. A scientific presupposition (climatic variations are cyclic and conveyed by the great general circulation of the atmosphere through the determine Stream); scientific goal (understand what, in turn, adjusts the movement of the great movement and the tropospheric flow). A model of scientific reference (the influence of the Moon on tides); a scientifically plausible intuition (the possibility that the gravitational force exerted by the Moon acts on air fluid as well as on the masses of water). Finally, a strictly scientific search to demonstrate, or refute, the validity of intuition.

Two luminaries of the sector, the physic–mathematical and computing of the University of Rome "La Sapienza" Alessandro Mei and the astrophysicist Mauro Dolci, participated on control calculations of physical–astronomical data. Thanks to their contribution, the intuition has become certainty: with its gravitational force, Moon influences the oceanic masses, but also the Jet Stream of the free atmosphere.

The various physical–astronomical gravitational formulas compared with calculations of physic–mathematical prediction models (this part of calculation and formulas will be disclosed in a next scientific dissemination), immediately showed an important correlation.

The idea that there could be an intimate relationship between the gravitational motions of the axis Sun–Earth–Moon and substantial changes speed and direction of tropospheric flow seems successful. A scientific detection able to radically changing meteorology and the concept of reliability of the prediction, amplifying precision and the forecast power not only in the middle–short but, even in the medium–long and very long period. By this discovery, once entrusted the "numeric grid" to powerful computing centers, today we would know the wheatear would be twenty years in any part of the world.

Going back to the question of a few lines ago: is it surprising? Same question, same answer: because in this case, the "revolutionary theory" has solid foundations in the past.

The dynamic that brings Sun and Moon to change the configuration of Jet Stream is linked to astronomical gravitational the law. In spite this science, astronomy, is in continuous evolution, the "basic" formulas that explain the crucial role of these two celestial bodies in climatic variations are known in centuries. There are three Kepler's laws and the Newton's law of universal gravitation.

Johannes Kepler (Johannes Kepler), German astronomer, mathematician and musician discovered empirically the laws that govern the motion of planets and that are called, in his honor, the three laws of Kepler.

The laws of the structure of the Universe are formed by studying the orbits of the planets in various solid figures, starting from Earth that is the unit of measurement for all orbits. Here they are in sequence.

9.5.1. *The orbit of every planet is an ellipse with the Sun at one of the two*
     foci

Applied to Moon's motion around Earth, this rule is *the orbit of the Moon is an ellipse with the Sun at one of the two foci.*

the Kepler's first law says that there are two points (aphelion and perihelion in the case of the Earth around the Sun, apogee and perigee in the case of the Moon in orbit around the Earth) in which the body taken into consideration will be closer (perihelion, perigee) or farer (aphelion, apogee) respectively to Sun or to Earth.

9.5.2. *A line joining a planet and the Sun sweeps out equal areas during equal intervals of time*

We can also think of the system Sun–Earth or Earth–Moon, it is the same, as with any other type of system with two bodies. The Kepler's second law explains that the orbital speed of the planet is not constant, but it is greater when the planet is located closer to the Sun, less when is more distant.

9.5.3. *The square of the orbital period of a planet is proportional to the cube of the semi–major axis of its orbit*

Kepler's third law learns that the greater distance of planet from the Sun, its periods of revolution are longer, according to a concrete mathematical relationship.

We shall now proceed to Newton and his law of universal gravitation. Sir Isaac Newton English mathematician, physicist, philosopher, astronomer, theologian and alchemist, is considered one of the greatest minds of all time.

Newton's law of Universal gravitation is a formula:

$$F = G\frac{Mm}{r^2}$$

Where G is the universal gravitation constant, M and m are the masses of the bodies were taken into account and r is the distance between the centers of the two bodies.

It is immediately evident that this force is closely related to the distance. More this distance increases, smaller is the force; and the relationship is exponential to the square of the distance. Even a small change in the distance, therefore, generates a considerable difference in the force taken into consideration.

By the formula of universal gravitation, we can get to the description of the gravity vector field. A conservative field that offers very useful information to clarify nature and mode of lunar action on the great general circulation of atmosphere. Through the gravitational vector field, is possible to calculate the force acting on a body by the force of gravity effect generated by a second body positioned at a certain distance:

$$g(r) = \frac{-GM}{r^3}r$$

With this formula, you can calculate the force exerted by a body of mass M on any point of the plane at a distance r from it.

If we unite Kepler's first law with Newton's the gravitation force and apply them to Earth–Moon or Sun–Earth system, it is evident that this specific force changes during the revolution of the two bodies taken into consideration. When the Moon is closest to Earth (perigee) exerts a greater force on the Earth surface, the same applies in the relationship between Sun and Earth.

This specific force is already well known for the effect that it exerts on tides (liquids), but it has never been taken seriously inconsideration in the study on Jet Stream's direction and intensity changes (fluid).

To understand the direct interaction that exists between Moon's gravitational force (observed through the Kepler and Newton's laws) and the Earth's movements, we have to consider frequent phenomenon: two tides, connected in time and space, with increases in sea level very different from the other just by the "position" of the Moon.

The lunar action on tides is predictable, foreseeing the lunar orbit. However, the orbit of our satellite has, in its unceasing procession, a myriad of micro–movements very difficult to calculate and to prevent. This is cause by a cross–action of gravitational forces between Earth, Sun and other planets of the Solar System, which complicates the situation and prevents a perfect mathematical calculation.

From this cosmic picture springs an orbital cycle not entirely pre-dictable, with a full rotation that occurs in about 18 years and half; after these years the lunar orbit backs in the same position.

9.6. Earth, Sun, Moon: menage a trois but Moon rules

Why does Moon and not Sun, that is bigger body, influence tides in this way (the tropospheric flow)?

The solar gravitational force is bigger than Moon's one (in fact Earth turns around Sun); but in this case, the really important element is a the variation of this force in the course of time, influenced by the proximity of Moon to the Planet. Moon makes its revolution around Earth in about 28 days, its gravitational force therefore varies much more quickly than the Sun's one and it becomes predominant. We find that solar tide weighs for a 46% with respect to the Moon, "quantity" certainly not negligible but secondary. Other bodies of the Solar System (Jupiter included) have an impact negligible on the tides phenomenon. The Jet Stream of the atmosphere seems to be subject to the same forces intersection that rules tides.

The solar the lunar gravitational forces are added or subtracted depending on the relative position of the three bodies (Sun, Earth, and Moon). This position depends on the lunar phase. The lunar phase gives precise information on the position of the Moon respect to Earth and Sun, allowing us to determine the angle that is formed among the three bodies, which is crucial to calculate the vector sum. In reality, Moon has an inclined orbit at approximately 5 degrees compared to the Sun–Earth's orbit plane. For this reason, we cannot fully take in consideration the lunar phase for this calculation.

There are two points, called "nodes", in which the three stars are perfectly aligned.

These "nodes" change their position, from month to month. For this reason, we must calculate this angular distance called "phase index" and identified with the astronomical term "elongation".

$$F = \sqrt{F^2_{solare} + F^2_{lunare} + 2F_{solare}F_{lunare}\,|\cos(elong)|}$$

It is therefore clear that during the phases of new Moon and full Moon, being the planets aligned the combined forces of Sun and Moon is bigger, while during Moon quarters it is smaller. At the same time, it is also evident that from month to month this force is affected by significant mutations, because the Moon is close or far, because Earth and Sun vary their distance, or because nodes are at different point. Using a simple combination of vector forces is possible to calculate the power the force at a certain point at given time.

9.7. The ruler stretches and draws the dress at the Jet Stream

The Jet Stream flows within atmospheric well–defined "levees", between 5 and12 km to average latitudes with the tropopause as maximum limit in height; and it is impossible that it raises or lowers, as tides do. This explains why the gravitational force acting on tropospheric flow not lifting or pushing it to the ground, but literally "stretching it" depending on intensity. So, forcing a significant change in terms of speed and direction and causing more prominent Rossby's waves and possible fractures.

At the same time, this clarifies the reasons for which in the tropical area there are no significant changes in the behavior of the Jet Stream, and on the climate: the gravitational force, in fact, here is almost completely perpendicular to the surface of Earth and it is ineffective on current at altitude, which cannot be lower or raise.

Insead, in the proximity of the poles or in temperate zone of Earth we have another situation. The lunar force has an important horizontal component and it generates elongations (parallel to the surface of Planet) of the Jet Stream.

We can say the same thing for centrifugal force, which has a primary role in liquid tide. It counteracts the lunar force and to generates the famous phenomenon of double daily tide. The centrifugal force, however, is more strong at the equator and it not exists at poles; and it is almost perpendicular to the surface of Earth: It does not contribute significantly to deform the tropospheric flow.

This explains the effect of the Moon on climate variations on Planet. Research on incidence of gravitational moving forces and on Jet Stream speed is recent, but we already have confirmation signals.

9.8. The past confirmation

This theoretical model was applied to past, superimposing the evolution of lunar phases to climatic ones, registered in the course of time. The coincidence was amazing. The comparison between the physical–astronomical data to physical mathematical ones, related to worsening weather recorded by meteorological archives, has found a correspondence with a very high statistical percentage.

We have analyzed periods from "negative record", such as the already–mentioned February 1956 or January 1985, by focusing the attention on "normal" years. These analyzes and comparisons revealed a correspondence of cause–effect between instability situations (or lasting stability) and the gravitational power induced by the Earth–Moon–Sun triad.

There are many mathematical astronomy data, but absolute values are particularly relevant. They indicate the maximum and minimum values achieved during the period analyzed, and the figure of elongation that identifies the Moon phases, the Moon–Earth gravitational force and Sun–Moon force.

For example, the absolute minimum was recorded in 2003, confirming as gravitational action Moon at historic minimum has created one of the hottest summers lived in Europe and in the Mediterranean area.

In those periods were recorded particularly high peaks of gravitational values or constant values of maximum action, active for a consecutive series of days or during ten days.

In short, all the times that, in the course of the past, this special lunar cadence was found, weather conditions are always marked for unusual virulence and persistent duration.

9.9. And the projections confirm

We have make a test, applying the same model to the future, to identify the moments in which specific changes in vector forces could unleash weather changes. We have obtained unimaginable precision future long range forecast. Confirming the "dominance" of the Moon on thermal vicissitudes, rainwater and Earth climate, and perhaps returning a lot of truth to some proverb of the old farmers or sea wolves.

We do not live in archaic age, but in the global communication and virtual era. Thus, maintaining a certain amount of caution on this discovery, waiting to be tested the validity, we have decided to apply this revolutionary model in forecasts and climatic projections, and put them on the web site www.meteoclima.net.

Visit it to believe, the projections issued during the year 2012–13 were always correct and the "real" climate event have had minimal deviations (a few days in early or late) respect to atmospheric progression predicted. It has happened even about forecast issued two months before. The physic–mathematical models (configurations of the great movement) have adapted to the forecast projection based on "lunar" physic–astronomical calculations: knowing Moon actions, we have predicted all changes of Jet Stream speed and the related configuration blocks, that before it was considered unthinkable.

9.10. Long–range forecast: the dream comes true

The gravitational research is just beginning and much more can be done to deepen it; but prospects are still outstanding. In fact, when the physical–astronomy grids will be entrusted to more powerful processors for physical–mathematical calculating (they already exist in some centers in the world), we will achieve an extreme precision forecast, e in the medium–long and in long period.

The computers programed with the solar–lunar gravitational forces will be able to prevent all variations in pressure at altitude, generated by vector forces: "mixed" to the physic–mathematical calculations these data will able us to anticipate the future actions of tropospheric flow. The weather projections will come to unimaginable levels of precision that today are impossible with the current methodology.

A historic step, it will allow to prevent the sequence of seasonal weather events, with millimeter precision. It allow us to identify multi–annual and annual weather patterns, but it will also give a formidable input to understanding of global climate change.

The lunar orbit oscillation seems really complex and unique, and its frequency of twenty years seems define that cyclic alternation of particularly hot and cold periods: the years '50–'70, cold; the years '80–'90, warm; and now the trend of years 2000, cold again. Everything seems to be connected to the Moon's behaviors.*

*Introduction and scientific articles of the world physicst and climatologist Dr. Clive Best (working in scientific research on Tides/Jet Stream) present on the page 154.

9.11. And even if it worked on the subject of earthquakes?

The research team Meteo Mundi, while focusing on the effects weather — the climate gravitational forces, has almost randomly opened a window on another delicate as fascinating issue. Working on physical–astronomical gravitational tables and projecting them on past, in fact, they found a clear correspondence between certain configurations of vector forces and seismic important events on a global and local scale. By analyzing the graph of the earthquake in Abruzzo or the most recent earthquake in Emilia, for example, was clear their correlation with contemporary peaks of gravitational forces.

If it was true, we would realized preventions, today completely unimaginable, on periods characterized by seismic risk. We cannot know "where" Earth will tremble, but we can have a projections on monthly and annual higher–risk that would provide a valuable opportunity to intensify monitoring, alert and prevent activities in critical areas.

9.12. Go forward in research: an objective, a duty

These scenarios, however, at the moment remain in the background, useful if to tickle curiosity of other scholars and to widen the catchment of attention and interest toward Madrigali Theory — Meteo Mundi.

The principle task of the Meteo Mundi team, at national and international level, and for now is to apply the best — on the field — the scientific instruments acquired to laying t foundations for a revolutionary line of research in meteorology climate and geology field. The first strategic step will be the development of a network of detection weather data at the forefront, with the installation of weather stations and innovative high technology. New Stations monitored and controlled, located in selected areas with painstaking precision, free from any anthropogenic interference and table to recording with accuracy the climatic effects of real Jet Stream on the weather of Planet.

The project, designed by Roberto Madrigali and Davide Peluzzi, with the precious collaboration, technology, computer science and design of Pier Luigi Caruso, will be linked to the further development of research on the great general circulation of atmosphere and on the role of Moon gravitational effects. It is based on professional monitoring of tropospheric flow, with constant and scientific analysis on the variations at altitude and its effects on the ground. We have baptized it with the name of *Meteo Mundi Project*.

Chapter X

Meteo Mundi Project

A global network of infallible sentries of safeguard human

Figure 10.1. Meteo Mundi Project, establishment of new developed weather stations.

Europe is a continent with different types of climate extending in latitude from colder regions of the North, beyond the Arctic Circle, to the temperate Mediterranean warm zones in South, close to North Africa; and in terms of longitude from Atlantic oceanic areas to the icy continental climate areas of Russian plains.

For this reason, the Old Continent there has extreme weather variability and a wide variety of climates and microclimates. In short, its complexity offers an almost complete phenomenal framework to scholars, proving a strategic observation and research field.

The marked and sometimes extreme shifts in weather conditions of recent years are causing (also in Europe) great political and economic difficulties, linked to the vulnerability of the human race caused by natural disasters and severe weather events marked and prolonged in time and space. Torrential rains,concentrated in a few hours, long periods of drought, sudden and lasting frost times: these situations heavily affect the local economies and global, causing geological hazards, damage to property, people, agriculture, tourism, and great difficulties in national and international connections.

Europe has the opportunity to develop a path of scientific research that will make it possible to predict in advance meteorological extremes, and therefore will make it possible to implement adaptation policies prior to reduce to disastrous effects, by adapting the natural systems and social traumas announced climate and their consequences.

This opportunity is represented today by the climate change research linked to Graet General circulation of atmosphere. The Madrigali Theory — Meteo Mundi has identified a direct cause–effect relationship between the flow movement in a

ltitude (Jet Stream) — maneuvered by the great movement and the polar Vortex with the decisive influence of the gravitational action lunar — and phenomena on the ground.

By monitoring the Jet Stream and researching on the polar Vortex expansion will be possible to identify the probable interference of the jet and decipher the future, by providing climatic cycles — in optimum as degenerative — and thus anticipating the extreme phenomena.

Essential priority at the global level on the study of Great general circulation of atmosphere, with gradual establishment of new developed weather stations will help researcher to relate the network of statistical data with real world information together with research and analysis of air (hot or cold) masses movement that influence Europe and the rest of Planet.

An efficient network is very important for the detection of the data and research on the great movement and it will allow us to predict weather and climate to implement an effective prevention of effects and disasters, planning the appropriate measures to contain them, preparing communities and their governments for any eventuality.

The collection of these data will begin from the only glacier in the Mediterranean area, the departure point of the network that will expand in different european climate strategic points and finally at the global level.

The main Goal of the project is to have access to a comprehensive statistical database with it identifying precise parameters of the relationship between what happens in altitude and what at the ground (between Jet Stream and the corresponding effects on the climate in the individual areas of the Planet); decisive instruments to develop reliable weather forecasts. These in turn will lead to better territorial schedules at regional level, but also to design a global framework of techniques, policies and preventive measures to help strengthen the ability to adapt and adjust their behavior — even with activities for the purpose of information and dissemination at all levels — to cope with any possible (indeed, more than likely) climate change future, momentary or lasting.

Climate change, as we have pointed out many times, are linked to the cyclical nature of penetration of the masses of air cold and hot at different latitudes, with specific cadence over the years and with a overwhelming importance of the masses of air polar, determinants in degencrative changes ends. For this reason a detection network is very important to monitoring penetration of arctic masses, both at high altitude and low latitudes, being the height fundamental point to observe the Jet Stream movements and the masses of air associated with it.

Italy and Abruzzo, the region where we have the Calderone Glacier on Gran Sasso d'Italia montain (the southernmost glacier in Europe), will play a fundamental role for the project. We will establish additional basis to monitoring equally strategic areas of the world: from Eastern Greenland to Himalayas, Siberia, Americas and Antarctica.

Local authorities, central agencies and scientific communities will have in this way, access to a dense network of statistical "certified and guaranteed" data, but also each individual community can realize, according to their specific interests or problems, adaptation actions in response to the potential impact of climate change on employment, investment policies, agriculture, and tourism. In short, may develop a overall governance aimed at quality of life of citizens, even in the case of extreme emergency.

Figure 10.2. Iceland, Vatnajokull glacier crossing.

To fully understand the importance of this project, its scientific accuracy, its potential contribution to the future of humanity and the collective duty to pursue its search path, now we also offer a short, but very clear, "technical basis".

The Meteo Mundi team relies the research with other collaboration researchers and glaciologists professionals. This group (Explora Nunaat International) has produced, through fieldwork, a painstaking documentation that confirms the theoretical pillars of the Madrigali Theory: a new cycle of cooling is started and there is a high incidence of tropospheric flow on climate change.

The climate informations comes directly from team Explora. The group, whose technical manager and president Is Davide Peluzzi, is an integral part of the process of scientific Meteo Mundi research and the related installation project of a network of weather stations on the axis Gran Sasso–Greenland–Himalaya. The arctic explorer's participation offers a great value contribution, since operating directly in strategic zones from the point of climate view. These researchers bring elements of concrete confirmation, real and not scientifically

Figure 10.3. Alps, ice.

questionable to Madrigali Theory. These "facts", are radically different from those that the whole world from for acquired due to the pressure media operated for decades by the prophets of the Global Warming. Empirical evidence that may appear "incredible", but in reality are simply ignored by the majority of climatologists and therefore omitted from the international information. Now we will explain what they have to tell us.

10.1. EXPLORA

Davide PELUZZI, Chief Explorer
Pinuccio D'AQUILA, Geologist/Glaciologist

After years of projects, research, human interaction and after you have received a welcome letter in reply from the President of the Republic Giorgio Napolitano on the need to "pacify" the world through the knowledge of nature, by means of the transmission and sharing of

Figure 10.4. Explora limits, http://www.exploralimits.com/.

knowledge between individuals, at the end of the year 2007 and is born the idea of a great project. Through a meeting of a group of friends, researchers of human knowledge, we realize a dream: the birth of the research group called Explora. It has the purpose to learn and disseminate, through the individual experiences, the knowledge of human knowledge. This is the challenge.

Our purpose is sharing and the knowledge of the wilderness areas of the Earth through the study of peoples "extremes" messengers of life on the planet.

Large spaces such as the Arctic, Himalayas, t Andes, Antarctica and Africa will be "our" places of research: the extreme lands.

Italy and Abruzzo, here is Calderone Glacier on the Gran Sasso d'Italia (the southernmost glacier in Europe), will play a key role, to monitor the status of expansion or contraction of the permafrost.

Meteo Mundi will be a point of reference for Italy and for the whole Mediterranean region. In fact, Calderone, positioned at a height of 2680 meters, is the southern offshoot Arctic in the Mediterranean with all the effects. The project will have various stages of progress and will include several areas of study and monitoring:

a) Gran Sasso D'Italia: the Calderone Glacier;
b) Eastern Greenland: areas over Ammassalik and Ittoqortoormiit joined to other strategic areas;
c) Himalayas: Nepal, Rolwaling Everest (installation of stations in very high altitudes, fundamental for the study of Jet Stream);
d) Enlargement to areas of national parks and international, as in Siberia, the Americas and Antarctica.

Il Presidente della Repubblica

Roma, 13 SET. 2007

Egregio Signor Peluzzi,

ho ricevuto la sua lettera, con il dettagliato programma delle iniziative culturali, rivolte in particolare agli studenti, sulle attività scientifiche ed esplorative svolte dall' *Ex-plora Nunaat* sui ghiacciai e montagne delle Alpi, degli Appennini e delle Regioni Polari.

Le esprimo il più sincero apprezzamento per tale opera meritoria di diffusione delle conoscenze naturalistiche e scientifiche, che assume particolare risalto per la concomitanza con l'Anno Internazionale Polare 2007-2008. In questi giorni in cui la questione delle Aree Polari torna alla ribalta per problemi irrisolti di delimitazione dei confini e di sfruttamento delle risorse naturali, ritengo che le vostre iniziative possano richiamare con forza – in tali zone come in tutto il mondo – l'esigenza di pacifiche intese e di una seria cooperazione internazionale.

Cordiali saluti

Ill.mo
Signor Davide Peluzzi
Via Risorgimento, 35
64046 Montorio al Vomano TE

Figure 10.5. Letter of thanks from the President of the Italian Republic Giorgio Napolitano to the team Explora Nunaat International.

Figure 10.6. Gran Sasso, Abruzzo, Italy.

Figure 10.7. a) Eastern Greenland; b) Himalaya; c–d) the monitoring of Glacier for a year, had its maximum September 2011.

Figure 10.8. Himalaya at sunset.

Figure 10.9. Antarctic, lawn of ice.

Figure 10.10. Gran Sasso, the Calderone glacier, end of September 2011.

10.1.1. *The Calderone Glacier, Gran Sasso d'Italia*

The monitoring of Glacier for a year, had its maximum in September 2011.

Gran Sasso massif, with 2912 meters of the Corno Grande, is a huge pyramid. In the center of the summit area there is a glacial cirque Calderone, exposed North East North, with morphological extension of 1 square kilometer. The affected area to glaciation is however restricted to a smaller surface (see photo).

The Calderone Glacier represents a particular morphological environment in which, thanks to its limited extent, we are able to appreciate and perceive the effects of climate in a sudden manner compared to apparatuses more extended.

This peculiarities, allowing you to detect even slight variations, however, generates often scare mongering by cry out to extinction, or vice versa to the expansion in the case of particularly favorable years.

These factor products the need to deepen the research in the area, both to contribute to the monitoring of parameters related to the mass balance and to weather variables, both to search for a correlation between the glacial oscillations and seasonal events.

Figure 10.11. Calderone photos sequence over the years 2005–2011 of the glacier and snow remaining.

This index may be able to indicate the evolution of morphological dynamics that may develop, for example in near areas. That areas covered by the glacier years ago, today have strong activity due to gravitaty phenomena and not only.

Understand the diachrony between climatic oscillations and trigger morfo–dinamic processes may represent the key to the defense of ground: environmental sustainability.

Calderone Glacier is a true natural laboratory, in the heart of the Abruzzo, for the study of climate. In addition to the glacier mentioned many other geomorphological forms (rock glacier and snowfields, permafrost etc.) and other massives, represent very sensitive indicators to climate change and have a considerable scientific interest. Further, Gran Sasso d'Italia (M. Pecci and P. The Eagle), often these forms, probably due to the different sizes, diacronically react at the same pulse climate and sometimes even seem to react in the opposite way.

Therefore, the special features of the environment of Abruzzo, which have a limited radius contrasts with morphological elements

Figure 10.12. Gran Sasso, spring 2013.

Figure 10.13. Iceland, Vatnajokull glacier crossing.

Figure 10.14. Gran Sasso, spring 2013.

Figure 10.15. Iceland, Vatnajokull glacier crossing.

with limited extension, allowing us to fully grasp even the most limited fluctuations.

Environments, such as the alpine glaciers, Himalayas or the Karakorum, respond due to their mass in a much more complex to fluctuating weather conditions. Moreover, these basins with very wide extension (see Baltoro, Karakorum, Pakistan), are affected by many other variables: the enormous difference between altitudes among (precipitation, temperature etc) the pelvis of accumulation and ablation, the different level of accumulation or exposure of the glaciers tributaries, etc. make much more complex their response to climatic oscillations.

For all these considerations, for its strategic location near the center of the northern hemisphere and in the Mediterranean area, we have chosen the Abruzzo and the Calderone Glacier as basis of the proposed studies carried out by the explorer Davide Peluzzi and the geologist–glaciologist Pinuccio D'Aquila.

By observing, in this area, the formation of new glacial nucleus to 2400 meters of Altitude on the vallone delle Cornacchie of Corno Grande, via the study by glaciologists–geologists of the Explora Team.

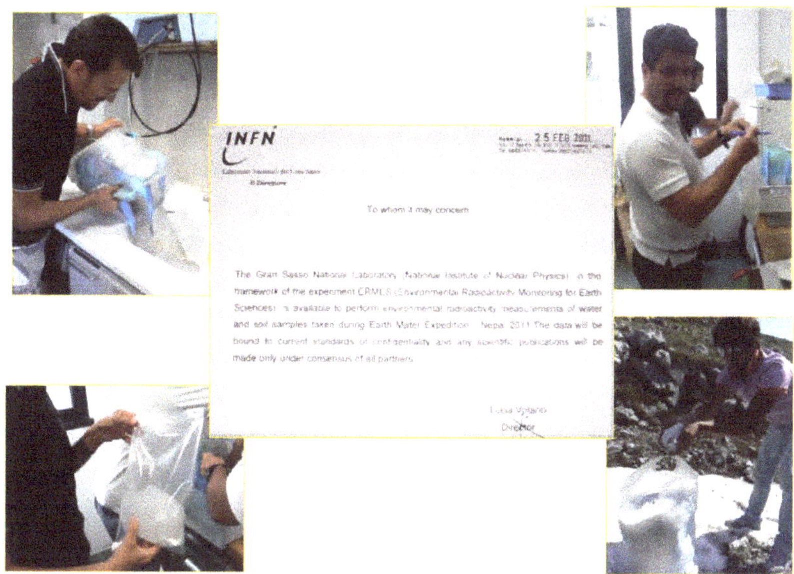

Figure 10.16. Hermes Experiment.

Figure 10.17. Gran Sasso, spring 2013.

In 2012 due to a single abundant snowfall in February and torrential rains in the month of July, followed by high temperatures in August, in the basal part is formed a sink, thus showing during the glacial deposit of more than 4 meters above the ice covered fossil debris of rock. On that occasion we carried out a sampling of ice and rocks in the basal area of the glacier, for the development of the experiment ERMES laboratories of the Gran Sasso.

The results are clear: the Calderone Glacier is in excellent health, the permafrost remains under ideal conditions, the contraction of the snowfields in 2012 is the result of contingencies specific already widely rebalanced by heavy snowfalls in 2013.

10.1.2. *Artic, Greenland, Iceland*

Greenland (in local language Kalaallit Nunaat, "the land of men"; in Danish Grønland, "green Earth") is an island on the American continent, the largest in the world for surface, located in the North of the Atlantic Ocean between Canada and Iceland.

The largest island in the world, Greenland, belongs geographically to North America.

The island is 8 times wider than Italy with 2,200,000 square kilometers and is covered for nine–tenths of an ice blanket. It is the widest mass of ice of the planet, second only to the South Pole.

Greenland has polar conditions. There are substantial differences, due to the amplitude of the territory, between the northern most area and the South of the island. The southern part has, in fact, a very mild climate in comparison to the inner zone of the country and in the north. In the center of Greenland is often record temperatures below –60 °C. The west coast and southwest, directed to the American continent and the hotter winds blow from it, offers the warmest climate of the island.

The thickness of the Inlandsis (the great ice cap) in some points is 3200 meters, Greenland and including 59° 40' and 83° 40' North.

The development of exploration during the shipments in Iceland on major glaciers (Vatnajokull, Snaffelljokul etc, in the years 2000, 2002); then in Greenland in 2006 and 2008 with shipments Gemini and Saxum monitoring and 2010/11, has allowed them to gain many environmental data. Temperatures, speed and direction of the winds, sam-

Figure 10.18. East Greenland.

Figure 10.19. Iceberg, Jamson Land, East Greenland.

Figure 10.20. Iceberg navigation photographed in East Greenland.

Figure 10.21. Iceberg photographed in East Greenland navigation of at least 70 m.

Figure 10.22. Iceberg, Jamson Land, East Greenland.

Figure 10.23. East Greenland, navigation difficult, Sermilik fjord.

Figure 10.24. East Greenland.

Figure 10.25. East Greenland and its unnamed peaks.

plings of ice, flora, rocks, and images of mountain peaks and glaciers explored (viewable in part on the web site www.exploralimits.com).

With the help and monitoring of various research organizations such as the DMI, the NOAA and others have observed especially in Eastern Greenland, the latitude of 66° north, that even in the summer, the Earth is protected by a belt of ice that leaves a few gaps and only for short periods.

To confirm this account climate, it is worth remembering that in the summer of 2008 the ship with food supplies for Tasillaq arrival only after 10 months of the previous, and the warehouses of the village were empty: this happened in July 2008.

It has been found that on the east coast also climbing is more difficult, in Greenland there are no roads and the closer to the mountains and built exclusively with boats or with expensive helicopters.

Extensions of the Arctic ice in month of April 2012

2012 was the period of maximum glacial arctic expansion during the winter–spring, as shown in the graph, followed by a contraction to the minimum levels in August–September. The latter fact is due to multiple factors, but are not related to processes of Global anthropogenic Global Warming. Importance is in fact the presence of the arctic fault with its active volcanoes that develops between the eastern Greenland, Iceland is the island of Jan Mayen to the geographic North Pole. The violent earthquakes of 6.6 Richter with epicentre in these areas, recorded in the August 2012, are evidence the presence of geothermal energy, in addition to the marine currents and their variables directions and solar activity.

Jan Mayen is a volcanic island located on Eurasian plate, of age fairly recent, dating back to about 700,000 years ago and on a hot spot that covers most of the mid Atlantic ridge. A part of such a backbone, called dorsal Mohns, terminates in the vicinity of the northern coast of the island and extends the fracture region of Jan Mayen 170 km toward the north–east, constituting a fault oriented to the north–west/south–east of the island.

A hundred craters to the multiple formats from trachyte and a dozen of eruptive fissures, have issued during the Pleistocene basaltic lava, which today composes most of the rocks on the island. The

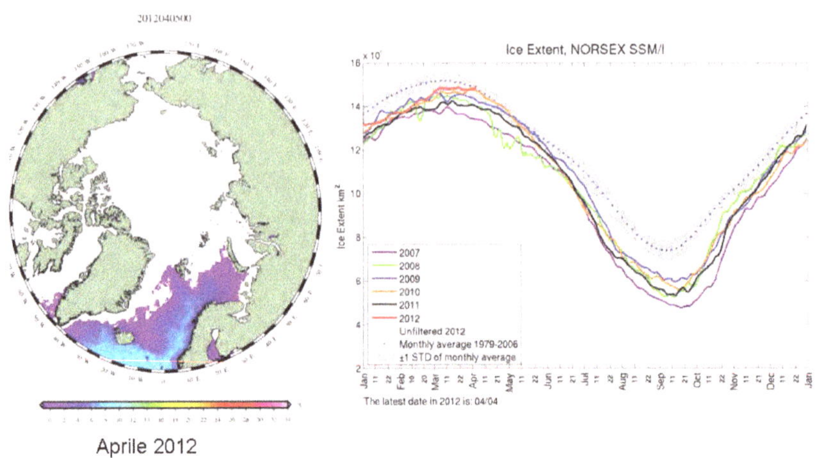

Figure 10.26. Ice Extent, April 2012, DMI.

rest of rock formation present on Jan Mayen was formed by debris transported by ocean current. The latter, in particular, has formed various small beads plains located mostly in the central part of the island.

The name iceberg derives from the Dutch word ijsberg which means mountain (berg) of ice (JIS), a term similar to Danish isbjerg, To German Eisberg, low saxon Iesbarg and Swedish and Norwegian isberg.

In italian, can be called icy mountain or, used very rarely, isbergo (adjustment proposed by the illustrious linguist Bruno Migliorini). In the past was said borgognone or ghiaccione.

The icebergs are the enormous detachments of Arctic or Antarctic glaciers (high also 170 meters above the water level, to consider that other 6 to 8 parts–volume are submerged). Postings occur for various reasons, but the main force is the formation of upstream ice of the trailing edge of the glacier. Other forces are due to variations in soil temperatures(geotermie–volcanoes) see Iceland or some areas of Greenland or Antarctica in addition to the seasonal variations of the

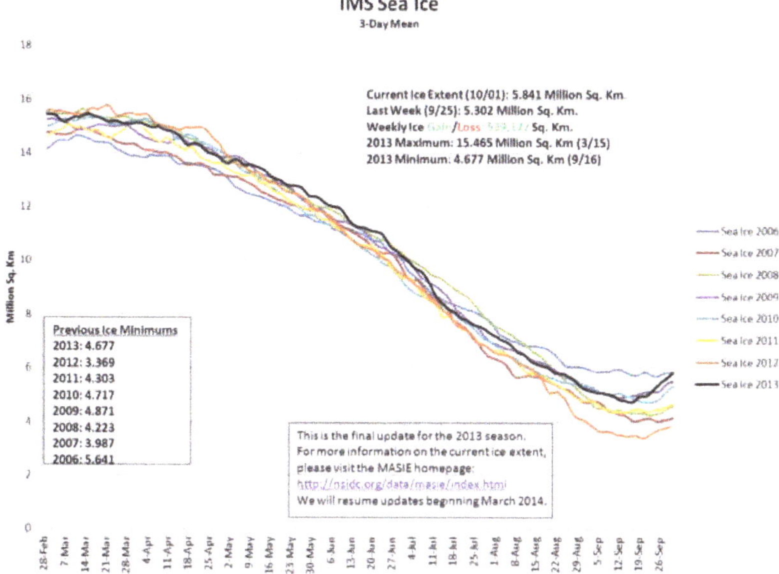

Figure 10.27. Ice extent 2013.

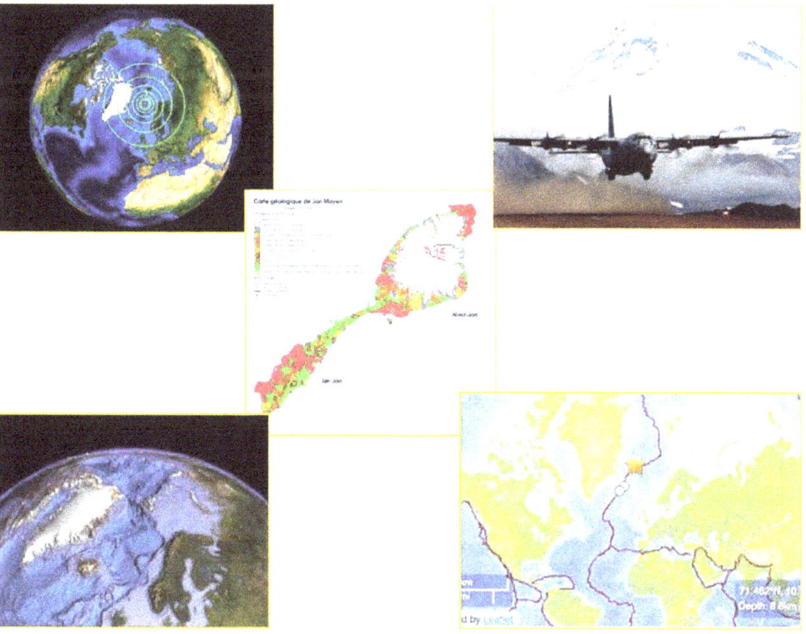

Figure 10.28. An earthquake of 6.6 R and Jan May. Volcanic island, geothermal energy.

Figure 10.29. Geothermal energy... Vulcanoes.

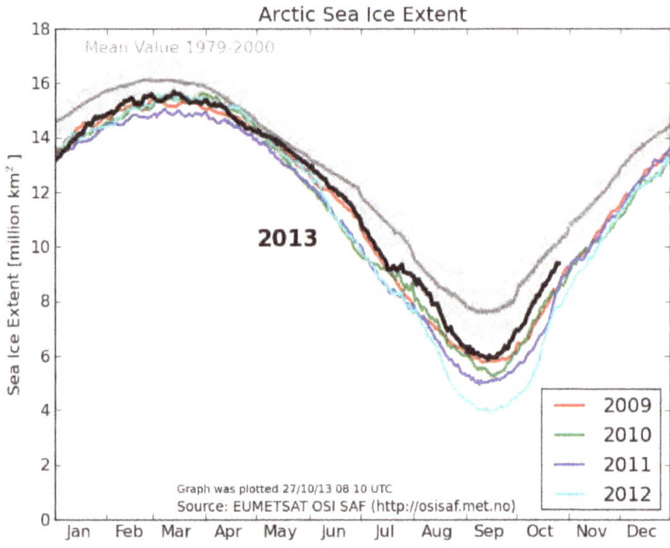

Figure 10.30. Extension of the Arctic pack that is revealing a strong expansion process, year 2013.

Figure 10.31. Structural differences between the pack and the iceberg.

climate. For example, in Antarctica that the internal temperature of the continent and on average in the summer to –30 °C and in winter touches the –70 °C and in addition, these postings are due to the aforementioned reasons. Remember that the water becomes ice at 0 °C, while the water of the sea has its solidification temperature to –1.8 °C. In addition, the color with the albedo, the soil has an impact on this phenomenon with the basalts Neri–Marroni, or the granite or limestone that differentiate this phenomenon of formation and removal, as well as for the seasonal variations of the climate.

The PACK and the formation of the ice above the mare:sull'Arctic Ocean (North Pole) and only Pack. The thickness is considerably lower than the Iceberg that reach hundreds of meters of ice fossil, while the pack on average is 3 meters — see pictures taken to the Arctic. Logically its dissolution and crushing depends almost entirely on sea currents and by underlying volcanoes, in relation to the seasons and solar radiation.

Figure 10.32. East Greenland fjord Sermelik–Inuit Fishermen on the pack.

10.1.3. *Himalayas, Nepal, Rolwaling Everest*

Himalayas the roof of the world also called the 3° Polo plays a fundamental role for the study of the climate and the glaciers of the Earth.

The snow, present throughout the year on himalayan landscape, is concentrated in the winter (especially under 5000 meters in height), with precipitation very abundant virtually anywhere: around 3000 meters, this season, the snow cover is usually thick about 3 meters. With the possible exception of special events due to, inter alia, variations in the atmospheric pressure, in the late spring himalayan, a large part of the territory has a snow cover of between 1 and 10 centimeters. Other areas more limited and circumscribed may submit covers between 10 and 25 cm and to a lesser extent between 25 and 50 cm. Even smaller are the areas where the accumulation of snow ranges from 50 cm to 1 meter in thickness, and focus (as with the other areas with covers more than 10 cm) in the north–north/west of the Himalayas, the most subject to snowfall.

Figure 10.33. The approach of the front with the arrival of the blizzard.

The expedition Earth Mater in 2011 in the region of the Rolwaling–Everest, has made possible the observation of glaciers in the said area. During the rise of the Parchamo (6300 meters), the glacial accumulations were remarkable. It was late spring and we found winter conditions by the thick layer of ice on the lake Tsho Rolpa approach has proven to 4500 meters to the icefalls to Beding, village at 3600 meters and the increase in the ice on the Tengi Rau Tau 6900 meters and to the surrounding mountains.

We have found greater accumulations than in the past years. In fact, the peasants Sherpa complained that low–altitude, in the years, the summer months had become colder, and then a smaller harvest of potatoes and grass for the Yak.

Also on the Himalayas in short, they do not seem to have adapted particular phenomena of heating. Indeed, were found not only unchanged climatic conditions compared to years past, but a degenerative extreme atmospheric situation, precisely in a period of rising to the mountains as the Parchamo or Melunghtze.

The shipment was in constant satellite telephone contact with the expert analyst physicist/mathematician and researcher on the climate, Roberto Madrigali, with regard to the monitoring climate weather of the area concerned to dispatch.

His precious and accurate advice with real–time monitoring, it has avoided secure and tragic consequences, at the time of climbing the Parchamo (6300 mt), for a violent storm of snow, which has been struck on the area as a whole (see satellite photo) for weather conditions in altitude (Jet Stream) that are atypical for the period.

Figure 10.34. Satellite photo which reveals the process of degeneration Atmospheric.

Figure 10.35. Himalaya, expedition 2011.

We owe to him and its recommendations targeted weather, if the group Earth Mater dispatch avoid prohibitive weather conditions. His prediction about advance a probable snowstorm in delicate time of the ascent at high altitude, has allowed us to get off in advance, thus avoiding cause–effect thermal and rainwater, which certainly have been tragic for the members of the expedition.

Himalayas, Earth Mater Expedition 2011

Zones from 4880 m of height, are characterized by temperatures consistently below zero (which determines the presence of perpetual snow) and twenty very intense. A unpredictable climate is changeable, with sudden snow storms, gales, floods and other phenomena. The winter has snowfalls very intense and regular, while in summer the climate is milder, although much more cold and the Tibetan plateau where there are average annual temperature of 1.1 °C and an average altitude of about 1000 meters.

The climate registered on the mountain peaks from 6000–7000 m and, to a greater extent, by 8000, hardly classifiable by virtue of the uniqueness of these territories.

In particular, the peaks over 8000 m are examples of alpine extreme climate: the average of winter temperatures and –36 °C, which may even, on Everest, at peaks to –60 °C. In June, the hottest month, there is an average temperature of –19 °C: zero is never touched nor passed to these altitudes.

The May 14, 2008 an Italian shipping has installed 8000 m at altitude, in the place of Mount Everest named Hill South, a weather station dedicated to Edmund Hillary. This meteorological station, in addition to being the highest currently working in the world, and connected with a network of weather stations, placed at decreasing altitudes, always in Nepal that will allow a in–depth knowledge about the meteorology of this areas.

Thanks to the excellent institutional relationship with the Nepalese Government team explore, we will try to give more force to Italian and international research.

In our group of research Meteo Mundi, posting in the weather stations project and JS, a detecting data in Himalaya, to monitor the tropospheric flow and its physical/mathematical variations.

To confirmation this, in 1951 Eric Shipton and Edmund Hillary, explored the area of the Rolwaling, documenting with precious images of mountains, at that time they have not name, such as the Parchamo or Melunghtze with the extension of their glaciers.

This expedition in Himalayas has allowed us to compare after 60 years images we captured in the expedition of 2011 with those of Shipton (book, "assault on the Everest") without encountering any significant difference of the himalayan glaciers as from attached photos:

Explora intends to contribute to a better understanding of the climate on the Earth through their shipments in extreme environments such as the Himalayas or the Arctic. This, in synergy with the studies of Explora state Roberto Madrigali, will seek to make someone else the "mystery" of climatic evolutions following a line of objective and free from bias research.

Eric Shipton 1953

Earth Mater 2011

Figure 10.36. The mountain Parchamo the unnamed Shipton.

Figure 10.37. This expedition in Himalayas has allowed us to compare, after 60 years, images we captured in the expedition of 2011 with those of Eric Shipton (in the book *Assault on the Everest*) without encountering any significant difference of the himalayan glaciers.

Conclusions

Catastrophic scenarios but no catastrophism a scientific research free from prejudice can protect life on Earth

The scientific report from journeys of the Explora team led by Davide Peluzzi, carried out in Greenland, Iceland, Arctic and the Himalayas, complete the work of Madrigali Thesis and closes the circle.

"The optical illusion" generated by hot twenty years of late twentieth century vanishes, and now we are in a new climate process. No anthropic Global Warming, the great machine climatic, closed a thermal cycle opens another one, addressed to cooling in the third millennium is manifested in progressive evolution.

From discoveries, the cooling process of Arctic is evident, even if for the moment in greater winter acceleration and summer contraction effect — as repeatedly pointed out — by the powerful geothermal action in progress under the ice: the concomitance of the solar maximum tends to compensate the increase of winter pack, by encouraging an energetic thawing process in summer.

The cooling process is, instead, much anticipated — and now from a few year — in Antarctica, where the enlargement of the pack and swirling is constant, with heavy weather impact on all the southern hemisphere. The facts, the real ones but that few people know, are evident:

— June 7, 2010. 500 African penguins die to the cold due to the cold wave that glacial has touched the Eastern Cape in South Africa;
— July 19, 2010. The glacial cold destroys in South Africa several hundred thermal solar systems;
— August 5, 2010. Snow on Brazil and sub–zero temperatures in River Plate. tropical fish death;
— August 6, 2010. South America is struck by a wave exceptional

cold. In Bolivia to the east down to –6 °C. Millions of fish are accustomed to swim at about 20 °C die frozen. The same happens to reptiles, birds and turtles. Therefore, the water becomes undrinkable and the government closes fishing for the entire year. The deaths of people and animals in Argentina, Uruguay, Paraguay and south Brazil increase. A meter of snow covers the Patagonia and along the Andes, you interrupt communications. Many Chilean cultures of citrus and avocado should be destroyed, reducing the export of 40%;

— August 9, 2010. Australians live the colder morning of the last 30 years. Sidney wakes up under a frost blanket;
— February 24, 2012. Rio Gallegos, Argentina: in summer –3.5 °C;
— February 26, 2012. Dome Argus, Antarctic Chinese station, there is a temperature of –64,7 °C, in the hot semester (austral summer);
— October 11, 2012. In Sydney an uniquely rare event, abundant snowfall in spring, when the temperatures normally here should oscillate between 15 and 20 degrees above zero. A few weeks before (September 2012) a sudden wave of cold takes snow in some mountainous areas of Santa Caterina, Brazil: in San Joaquin and spring but it snows for almost two hours, with a temperature of 2 °C below zero. In San Paolo (Tropic of Capricorn) down to an incredible +6 °C;
— 2012/2013. The average extension of the Antarctic pack passes the winter record and in the first half hot records an increase much greater than the average thirty years (charts);
— 2012/2013. The average extension of the arctic pack exceeds the values over the past 10 years (graphs).

The expansion of the pack, to the north and south of planet, will unleash in the coming decades a significant decrease in global temperatures. This thermal effect is shall declare with ever greater emphasis in the years to come, and soon will be felt throughout its virulence in the northern hemisphere. The percentage ratio of the albedo effect will increase for the reflection generated by Arctic and Antarctic pack and will be a key factor in promoting a cooling process increasingly intense. The vitality of Polar Vortices, responsible for pejorative situations moving toward lower latitudes, will reinvigorate her to turn the process.

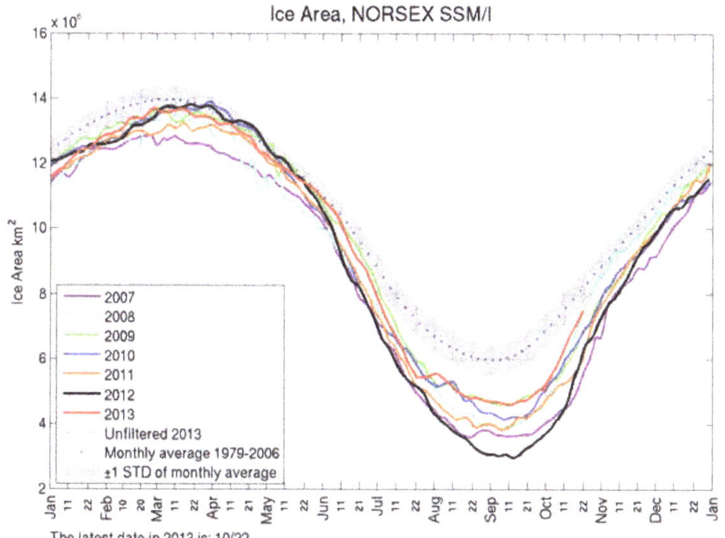

Figure 10.38. The process of increasing the pack in the Arctic.

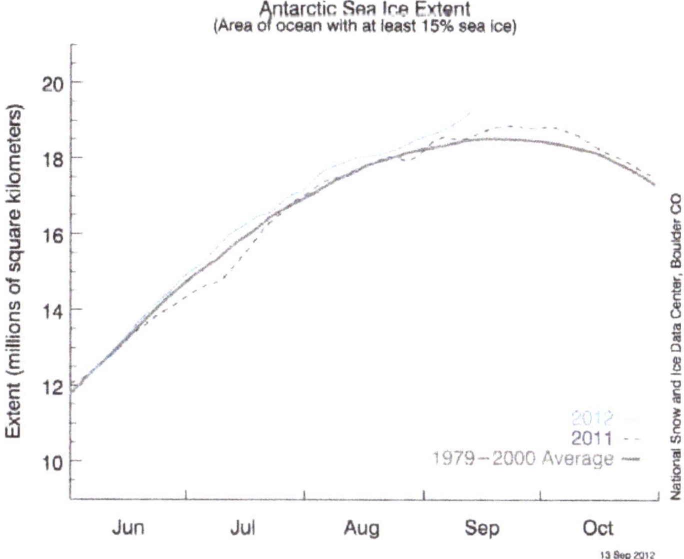

Figure 10.39. Chart of the Antarctic pack that reveals its growing increase denying the anthropogenic GW.

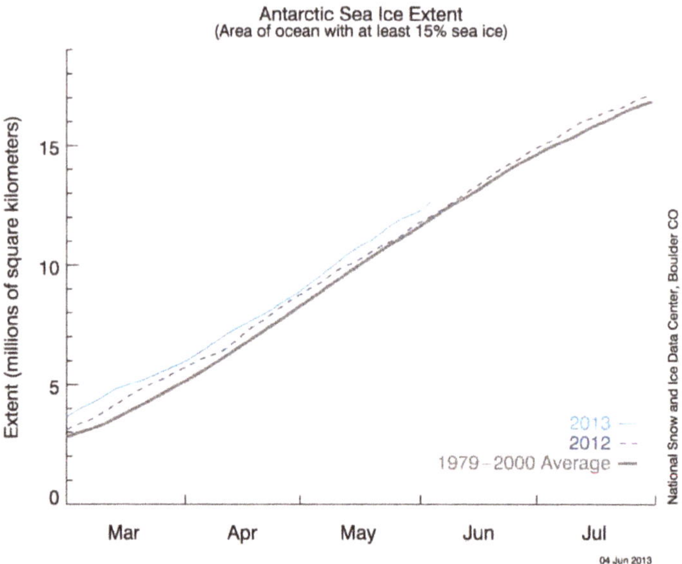

Figure 10.40. Chart of the Antarctic pack that reveals its growing increase denying the anthropogenic GW.

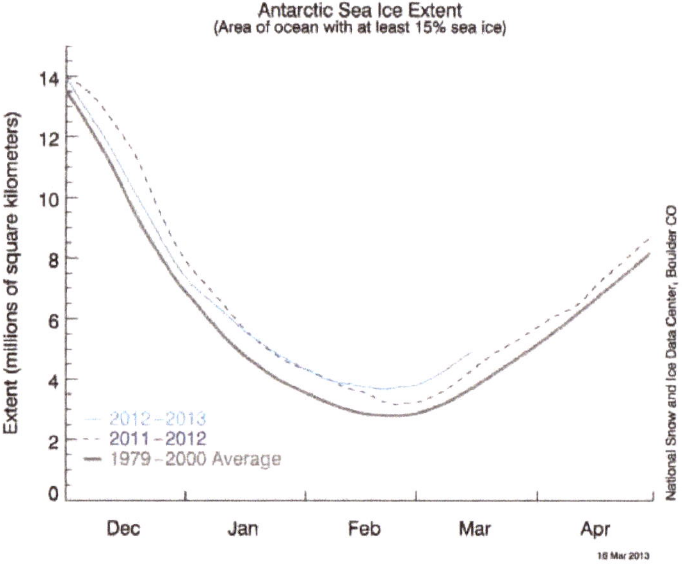

Figure 10.41. Chart of the Antarctic pack that reveals its growing increase denying the anthropogenic GW.

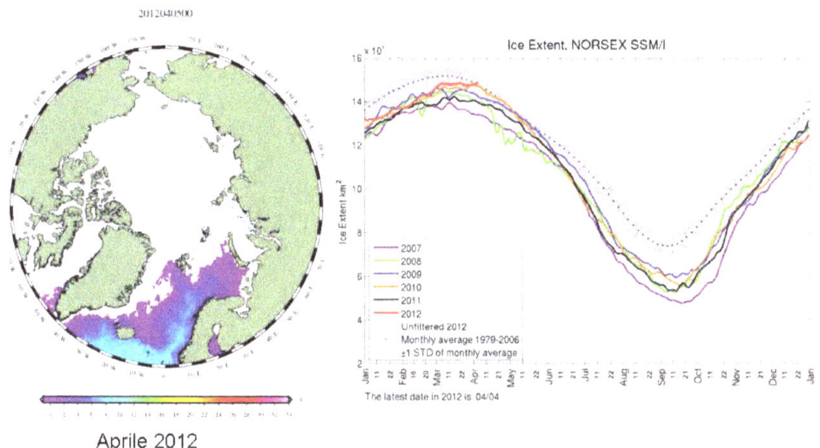

Figure 10.42. Ice Extent in April 2012, DMI.

The observation of these recent winters detects a drastic increase in precipitation and snowfalls record. Even in the "half north" of the planet, as evidenced by what is happening for some time now in North America, Asia and Europe, in:

— December 22, 2011. Historical event: glacial increase on the east coast of Greenland, a bridge of ice joins the Greenland Iceland;
— winter–spring 2011–2012. For the extension of the arctic pack, for the first time in decades, reaches and exceeds a little the average thirty;
— January 16, 2012. Extraordinary Wave of cold in India. New records of absolute minimum at Nizamabad (Andhra Pradesh), 4.0 °C; in Mysore (Karnataka) 7.7 °C. The same day in Bangalore 7.7 °C, the lowest temperature of the last 19 years in January;
— January 17, 2012. New record of absolute minimum to Greek station of Florina, 643 meters of height on the sea, on the outskirts of West Macedonia. The thermometer in hellenic town

drops up to –25.1 °C, destroying more than 3° the previous record of absolute January 6, 1993 with –22.0 °C;

— 27 January/17 February 2012. A terrifying cold wave engulfs part of Europe and North Africa, killing more than 650 deaths in the affected areas, from Russia to Greece (only in Italy 57 confirmed deaths, 48 in Algeria);

— November 2012. In the early days of the month, exceptional and early snowfall in New York, with accumulations of more than 12 centimeters: beats the record dating back to 134 years before, November 1878;

— December 2012. Christmas nightmare in Russia, roads, and highways blocked by ice, at least 123 confirmed deaths, temperatures at –30° to Moscow, beyond the –60° in Siberia. In Tuva (border with Mongolia) 3000 people are evacuated because it is impossible to heat in any manner the dwellings;

— January 4, 2013. In South Korea (same latitude of the North Africa), the columns of mercury fall steeply, –16.5 °C in Seoul, the minimum 27 years;

— January 9, 2013. 15 centimetres of snow on Jerusalem. Has not happened for at least twenty years. On the same day snow at low altitude even in very hot Lebanon. Still record cold in India, the airport of Patna with 1.1 °C, at Bareilly with –0.1 °C (previous record 0 °C in February 1905);

— January 12, 2013. The Bangladesh authorities reckoning of the wave of frost in the course of some days, the number of confirmed deaths are 90;

— January 23–24, 2013. Frost seized the United States. In Chicago –46 degrees and incredible images are on a tour of the world. Burns a factory, the water thrown by the hydrants of firemen for extinguishing the fire freezes instantly;

— March 12, 2013. Cold and snow: a new wave of bad weather "Siberian" strikes the North Europe. Roads become paralyzed, canceled flights in Belgium, France, and England. Discomfort even in Germany, where the Frankfurt airport is closed. Suspended the Eurostar between Paris and London. The most critical situation in France: more than 68,000 houses in Britain and Lower Normandy without electricity due to the heavy snowfall. In half of the country no highway and practicable.

These lists of dates and facts, relating to both the right and left hemispheres, are incomplete. In fact, they appear, together with another cyclopean mole of similar information, on dozens and dozens of Internet sites, skilled and unskilled. But did you know them, apart the most famous cases?

The curious aspect of matter is that on "cold cases" the international media are silent, or li tell how accidental phenomena. While great attention is given to news of opposite sign, verified or not: if in Greenland a year dissolves a portion of ice to make way for the grass (and geothermal activity?) this becomes a conclusive proof of Global Warming. On the other hand, that the Antarctic pack for ten years advances to rhythms ever encountered in the past, or that the Russia (Russia!), for the first time, find out that its highways are not cold–proof, well, this is ignored or it means nothing.

The reason for these singular disparities is simple. The climatic extremes, with relative temperature peaks upwards or downwards, are frequent; both in a cooling cycle that to in heating cycle. While a hot record does not invalidate the theoretical framework of Madrigali Theory (indeed, underpins the crucial importance of configurations of the Great general circulation of t atmosphere in the effects to the ground on specific areas and microclimates), cold records of the past few years and the expansion of pack represent an insurmountable obstacle to the hypothesis Global Warming. If in fact it was a progressive and irreversible global warming, localized in contrast phenomena would be inexplicable. Unless, as unfortunately happens, using theories about increments of cloudiness and rainfall.

The progression in acceleration of the climate toward cold and instead made more evident by the intrusion of winter in the intermediate seasons. Shrinks the summer period and "widen" the intermediate seasons to start from high latitudes. There are very stormy springs, with extreme temperatures both upward and downward, and summers atypical and suffering toward the medium high latitudes, except side effects and transient in contrast, species in the Mediterranean.

What does it mean? First of all that, contrary to what you think, the planet today is cooling down. The anthropogenic pollution, therefore, poisoned the nature and the living species, but does not affect the climatic cycles, influenced instead by the Great terrestrial climate machine on which man has no faculty, in good and bad, of intervention.

If we were in fact in the midst of an interglacial era, respecting time and mode of the great machine climate we could reasonably expect that current process of global cooling is completed, between high and low, in the "usual" lap of 18–20 years that has characterized the planetary climate swing over the past few centuries.

Now, however, humanity sits on the edge of a precipice announced, however, is here from all ignored, removed, deeply critical: the era interglacial that has encouraged the birth and development (in the "better air–conditioned" geographical areas of the Planet) of the great civilizations of which we are heirs and continuers of, is closing. Indeed, and peters out. The 11,500 years that nature — from time immemorial — the has cyclically assigned to intersperse the large and infinitely longer glaciation, are practically exhausted. If Earth obeys the rules that have governed here for millions and millions of years, in the short will be his entrance, the new, unavoidable, glacial era.

Anyone who is here today, has the possibility to not being there, that day. But there is the concrete possibility the generations to us nearby, children, grandchildren or great grandchildren will be alive for dangerous rendez–vous with perennial ice lies in. It is a devastating prospect.

In fact, if a hypothetical global warming with the consequent seas raising of the would cause, in the worst case, the uninhabitability of precise geographical areas (saving at least the greater part of the land habitable), the great ice would cancel instead every assumption of social life, at least as we know it today, in most of the world. Favorable conditions for agriculture and livestock farming (and therefore to the supply of food) and the normal economic activities (travel, trade etc.) with the advent of the glacial era will only in the equatorial tropical and subtropical zones. For example, in the Mediterranean basin you would equate as today in same areas of Greenland. The rest of humanity will live as Eskimos.

Certainly, some man will say, in Greenland you live, so how can we live in Siberia or the North Pole. It is possible because in those so cool places are settled only small communities, that survive with few resources and consumption and is still closely linked to what they receive "from the rest of the World", both in terms of technology and food. If we invert the proportion, if should be the "small" equatorial community (with its narrow portion of available territory) to ensure

Figure 10.43. The scenarios open by a new ice age.

the survival of the billions of people who crowd the continental areas today, that tomorrow will be icy — the unsustainability of the system would be truism.

The scenarios open by a new ice age, in short, are appalling in relation to the complexity reached by the global social system and the record amount of inhabitants of Earth. We were interested in the "psychological terrorism" as a useful tool to draw attention to our scientific theory, or maybe to make this book a profitable best–seller, we could draw prospects even more catastrophic than those by which Global Warming theory has built its success.

We could hit by relying on collective fear. But, we prefer leave these fascination techniques to others.

The Madrigali Theory — Meteo Mundi is limited to observe facts, trying to predict the consequences, to turn on an alarm bell and to suggest those that, according to the scientific facility on which it is based, may be the best defense strategies against a big problem, inevitable, but fortunately announced.

The facts, and we have them listed, these are:

a) pendulum which scans always gives the climate evolution of the planet Earth, and at the apex of an oscillation (an era interglacial with its favorable climate to human presence) and starts inexorably to fall toward the other, one hundred thousand years of ice age, the whole hostile to all forms of life;

b) the next, closer and, glacial era was not enter "tip–toe", according to a slow and gradual gait, but suddenly and violently erupting triggered by a particularly cold time cycle (a few tens of years) at the summit of which the "Earth system" will no longer capable of rectifying and precipitate at exponential rate toward frost;

c) from 10 years, contrary to the Global Warming thought, on the planet is records exactly this potential and formidable assumption: a cooling period is starting and is developing rapidly; it is very strong and insistent especially in Antarctic regions;

d) as there is no available tool to the human kind to unleash a process of global warming, in the same way nothing on Earth can stop the triumphal march of the frost.

It is quite impossible, in the current state of knowledge experience, say if it is happening to the global climate in the Third Millennium, the cooling in progress, is the prelude to the new ice age, or only one of the last "secondary oscillations" that characterize the climate variability of each interglacial era.

The Madrigali Theory and Meteo Mundi Project however offer to the scientific community a new perspective, based evidence plausible data, by which observe the phenomena in act to reach a deeper understanding of mechanisms that determine them and the possibilities to predicting evolution.

Thanks to the recognition of the crucial role played by the Great general circulation of atmosphere, through the Jet Stream and the Polar Vortices, we can now understand why and how the effects of climate change manifest on the Planet.

On the other hand, the revolutionary discovery of the decisive influence played by gravitational lunar forces, with their cyclic cadence, can tell when these climate changes will manifest themselves with greater or lesser virulence, in near and far future.

In short, using configurations of the tropospheric flow and the grav-

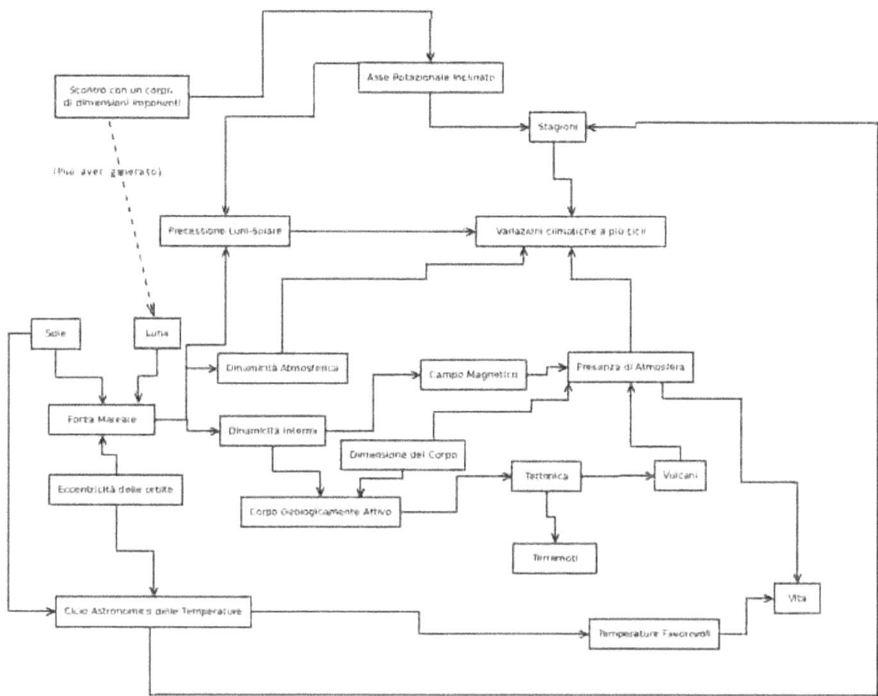

Figure 10.44. The revolutionary discovery of the decisive influence played by gravitational lunar forces.

itational variations,we could at least get to predict with good advance critical moments with greater risk of extreme climate), including the dreaded moment in which with great probability the balance will shatter and the ice age will start.

To make that this perspective becomes a reality, we do not need colossal and international investments or plans (such as, for example, the Kyoto Protocol, which due to its cost remains alas almost go un-applied), but the "simple" targeted actions suggested by Meteo Mundi Project: implanting a planetary well–made network of detection, then enter the data obtained by this network in powerful computers able to overlap with the evolution of lunar orbits.

It will be possible to develop long–term global weather forecasts and with absolute accuracy.

It is clear, as we now have repeated almost to exhaustion of our readers, this will not however to stop, to deflect or even only to influence, the "natural desire" of the great machine terrestrial climate and its inevitable paths. In the face of this will be possible only defend themselves.

When you are forced to play defense the ability to predict the moves of the opponent becomes however vital. For this the abandonment of the misleading "Ptolemaic dogma " of Global Warming (or at least the willingness to put it in debate to al–low other theories to verify its reliability), today desirable and obligation of science, in front of the irrefutable cooling process in progress, and the equally indisputable "agony" of the interglacial in which hitherto we had lived.

The input of a very cold weather period be it temporary or "final", requires a extraordinary, planetary mobility.

Must be reviewed, and with great anticipation, the rules themselves that today govern the majority of human societies, especially those more advanced that they may find themselves "mutilated" precisely in their technological foundations.

Faced with the glacial prospects, every single local community will have to adapt, while the international community will have to start large emergency plans.

Paradoxically the "spectrum" (concrete!) of the great cold — a mirror what has become of the nightmare of the great heat in relation to environmental issues — could induce beneficial global reflections on the balancing of the relationship between the "North" and the "South" of the world, because they will be exactly the latter to ensure the survival of the human species.

In addition you will have to accelerate the process of research on alternative energy, because you will multiply to the infinite, the demand for heating fuel, the forested areas exploitable will reduce death throes and the oil resource is far from inexhaustible.

Without taking account of the obligation to preserve this immense biodiversity heritage (about 75 per cent of the living species) that the big cold would cancel for ever.

The development of the Madrigali Thesis — Meteo Mundi Project shows itself, in the short term, in "small daily things": Which socio–economic benefits could produce a simple weather forecast in the medium term? Is it able to say precisely to a farmer, a viticulturist, a tour operator or to an organizer of major events en plein air if his next season will be marked by hot, cold or rain?

From tangible daily advantages to a possible defense of humanity in the face of a catastrophic ice age: the path begun many years ago with the first steps of Madrigali Theory that today it is wide–open motorway on a possible scientific revolution. Science, and to all those who have the right to make important decisions, have the task not liquidating it in the name of dogma and prejudice. Have gotten curious, reflect, take responsibility. The effectiveness of meteo–climatic forecasts based on madrigal Theory is established. The decisive leap forward, that can change the world, is near.

Earth's future is written in a great mechanism of the air and in the Moon. To read it just raise our eyes. And don't expect you renunciations on behalf of certainties that for its good statute the science does not admit, but open you to the dialog with who has raised the eyes and invites — as Galileo 500 years ago — simply to experience. The stake is huge: it's not worth it?

THE RESEARCH OPENS ABROAD AND IS ENHANCED BY THE ENGLISH PHYSICIST DR. CLIVE BEST

We went ahead in scientific research, experimenting with the physical and mathematical calculations with variations of Tides, getting satisfaction and confirmations ever more rewarding.

The objective of this book in the English version, in print and digital in its first draft, is to encourage a wider diffusion of the research, involving foreign users, and to stimulate and intensify the interest and discussions on the web.

From this opportunity is born the collaboration in research on the Tides and Jet Stream with physicist and climate expert Dr. Clive Best, a BSc in Physics and PhD in High Energy Physics and worked as a research fellow at CERN for 3 years, Rutherford Lab for 2 years and the Jet Nuclear Fusion experiment for 5 years.Thereafter worked at Join Research Centre in Italy until April 2008 being seconded to the African Union in Addis Adaba November 2007 until March 2008.

Clive is interested in understanding the physics behind climate change tired to hear that the debate is over. Science is never a closed book, and has a habit of turning around and biting those who think so. This explains why the blog now focuses on climate science.

Enthusiastically Clive is in this second draft of the book in English and enriches the scientific part of further research on the tides and the effects on the Jet Stream> Polar Vortex publishing some of his most authoritative scientific articles performed during our collaboration to study and scientific research.

With Clive, thanks to shared ideas, was born a valuable and prestigious collaboration that is stated even further in this publication. Physicist and climatologist expert, Clive Best works with the most authoritative international organizations, he writes on the main blogs and he is in touch with the most influential experts in climate in the United States and the United Kingdom.

On his influential blog on climate science you can find articles published in the book, along with many other interesting articles http://clivebest.com/blog/?page_id=6055

Hope you enjoy reading about these scientific and popular articles chosen by his blog and about our foreign cooperation on the study and research weather and climate change commanded by the Tides and Jet Stream.

DOES THE MOON AFFECT THE JET STREAM?

Posted on July 4, 2014 by Clive Best

Evidence is presented showing that lunar tides do have a significant influence on the strength and position of the polar Jet Stream. The Jet Stream drives northern latitude weather patterns especially during winter months.

I was intrigued by a proposal made by an Italian meteorologist Roberto Madrigali that varying tidal forces during the lunar cycle change the position of meanders (Rosby waves) in the polar Jet Stream. He has also written a book on the subject. This winter saw stormy but mild weather in the UK with exceptionally cold weather over North America. Both were likely caused by large distortions in the Jet Stream. Does the moon's ever-changing tidal force affect Rosby gravity waves in the polar Jet Stream? The hypothesis, put simply, is that atmospheric tides acting just below the stratosphere affect the flow of Jet Streams. Increased tidal forces pull the Jet Stream to lower latitudes thereby inducing the mixing of polar air with tropical air. The result of such forcing is an increase in waves and oscillations in the Jet Stream and lower pressure differences.

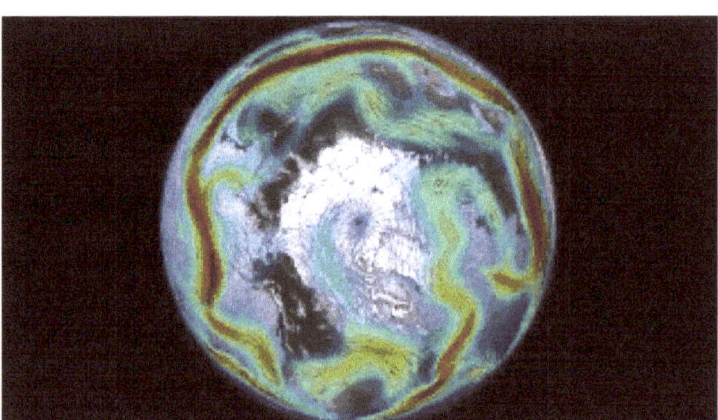

Jet Stream animation

One indicator of how contorted the Jet Stream becomes is the measurement of the difference in pressure between the Icelandic Low and the Azores High. There are two indices used to do this–one called the Arctic Oscillation (AO), which treats the flow over the entire Northern Hemisphere, and another called the North Atlantic Oscillation (NAO), which covers just the North Atlantic. The two are closely related. When these indices are strongly negative, the pressure difference between the Icelandic Low and the Azores High is low. This results in a weaker Jet Stream with large, meandering loops, allowing cold air to spill far from the Arctic into the mid-latitudes.

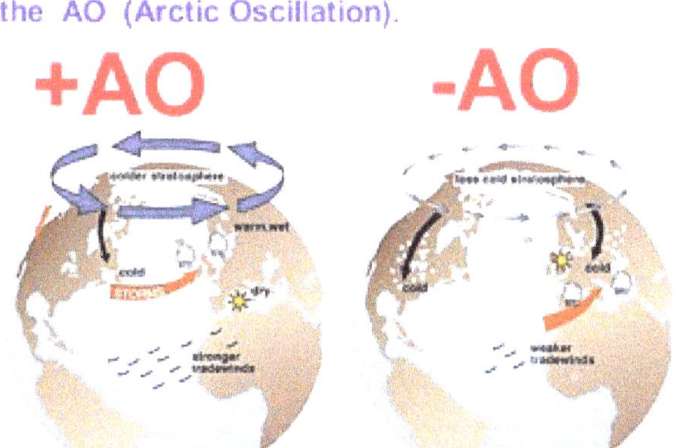

Schematic of Arctic Oscillation

Severe UK winters such as those in 2009/2010 and 2010/2011 coincided with strong negative values of AO/NAO , whereas the mild but stormy winter of 2013/14 coincided with strong positive values of AO/NAO. The Jet Stream influence on Europe is stronger during the winter. This is also the time when solar heating of the atmosphere is diminished over the Arctic, so any possible lunar tidal effect will be enhanced.

To investigate further the hypothesis of a lunar influence on the Jet Stream I downloaded the data from NOAA and calculated the net tides for each day from 2000 until 2014 using the JPL ephemeris. I am basing these calculations on the formulae derived in <u>Understanding Tides</u>*1. Figure 1 shows the AO and NOA during the interval plotted together with the net solar/lunar tidal acceleration.

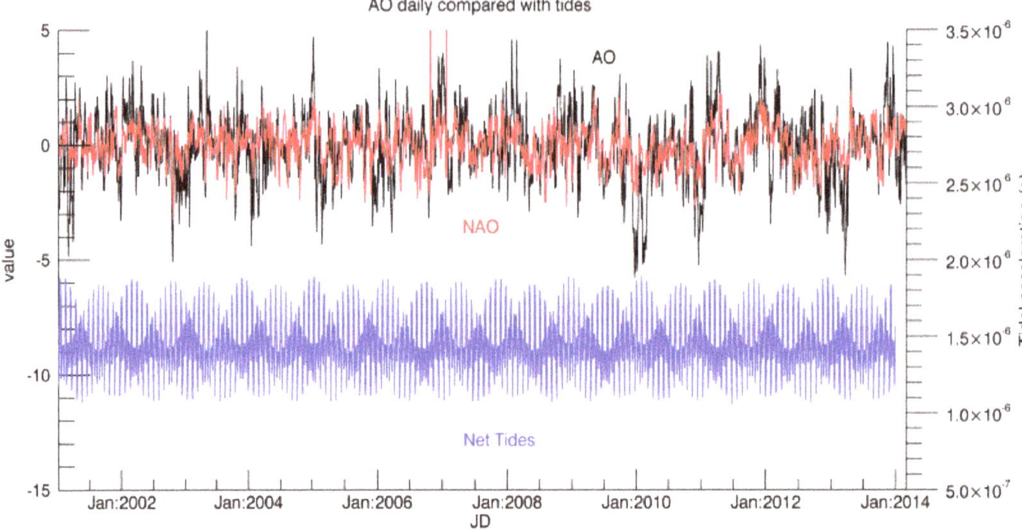

Arctic Osclilation (AO) and North Atlantic Oscilation (NAO) indices. Shown in Blue is the net lunar-solar tidal acceleration from 2001 until 2014. It is seen that in general the AO and NAO agree with each other so we simply now concentrate on the AO data. The period of oscillation of both is indeed similar to the monthly change in lunar tides, but no obvious cause and effect stands out at this level. We now look in more detail at two years of data: 2003-2004.

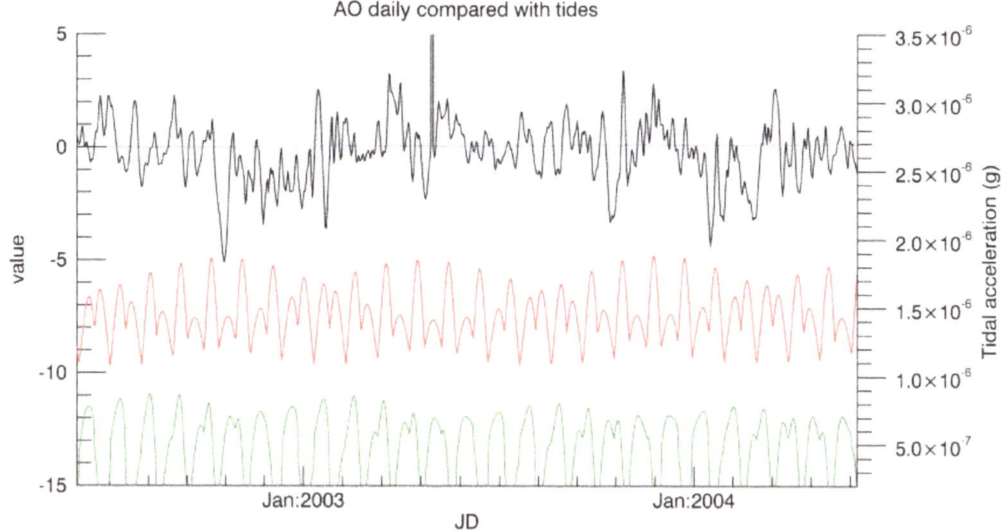

AO compared to net tides and the lunar tractional component at 45 deg. 2002 until 2005. The lower green curve is the tractional component of tides (see below)

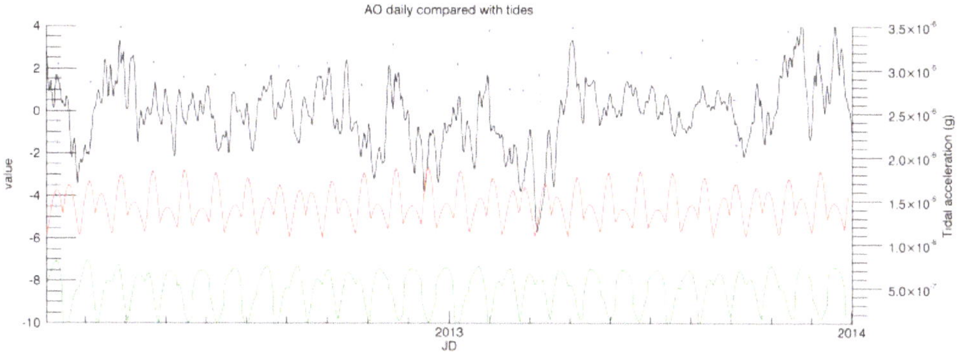

Detailed look at the last 2 years of AO data

Intriguingly the oscillation period of the Jet Stream is also around one month. However there is only a small 3% anti-correlation between net tidal forces and AO. This gives just a hint of a tendency that when tidal forces are large the AO tends to go negative. The largest apparent "atmospheric tides" are those due to solar diurnal expansion. These are not gravitational tides.

During northern winters such "solar heating" is diminished over the Arctic. Winters are the period when lunar gravitational tides could be expected to play more of a role in the positioning and strength of the Jet Stream, if such an effect exists at all.

I therefore decided to look more closely into the latitude dependence of the lunar tidal forces and in particular at the horizontal component of the tide or traction. It is this component which can move water and air long distances during the tidal cycle. Its strength varies during the lunar month and during the 18.6 year precession cycle. I calculated the tractional force/unit mass or acceleration for 60N and 30N which covers the range in latitudes typical of the Jet Stream.

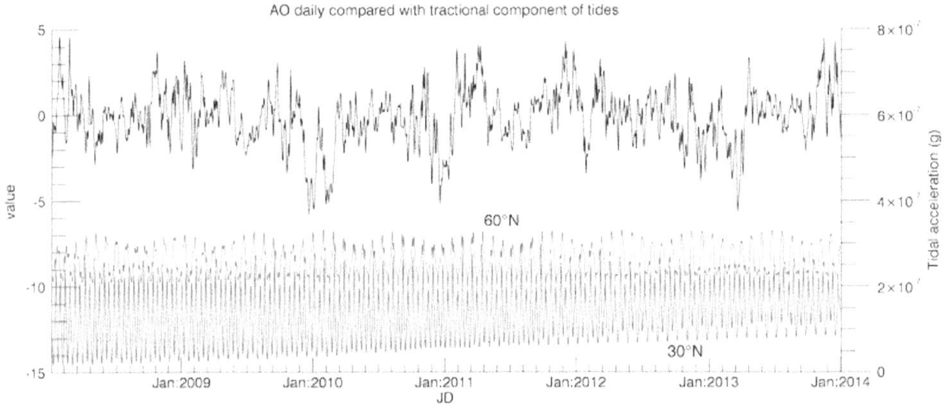

AO compared to the tractional component of tides for latitudes 60°N and 30°N. Note how the range of forces varies with the changing moon declination after the maximum in 2007.

What is particularly interesting here is the dependence of the tidal force on the 18.6 year precession cycle of the lunar orbit. The maximum standstill of the moon was around 2006-2007 when the declination angle reached a maximum of 28.6°. Since then it has been declining and is currently around its minimum value of 19.5°. A high declination angle actually reduces the tractional force most evident in the 30°N value shown in green above. There have been several papers reporting a link between the 18.6 year cycle and droughts across the US and central Asia. If the moon really is affecting the Jet Stream then this could be the explanation.

Winters 2010 and 2014

Now we look in detail at two winter periods. Firstly the harsh winter for the UK in 2009/2010 which corresponded to low values of AO. Is there any evidence for a lunar tidal effect on the Jet Stream in winter ?

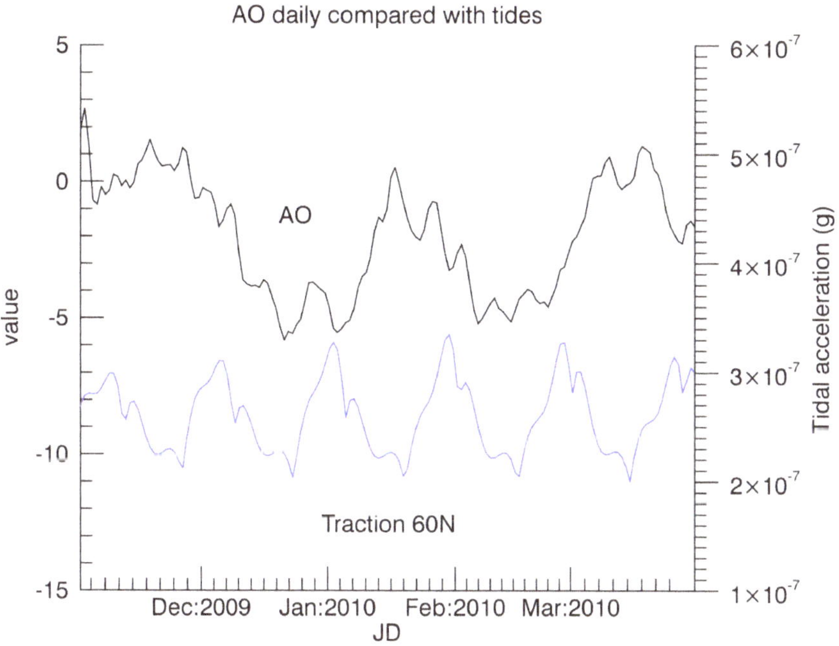

Winter 2010. Clear causal relationship between tidal traction 60N and the AO.

I find this result remarkable. It shows clear evidence of a relationship between the strength of the lunar tidal force and the positioning and strength of the Jet Stream. There is an underlying anti-correlation showing a reduction in AO with tractional force at 60N even matching some details. There must also be a stochastic component so the agreement cannot be expected to be exact. Finally we look at last winter 2013/14 which saw the Jet Stream meander further south bringing storms to the UK. Since the meanders of the Jet Stream reached down to lower latitudes, I calculated the tractional forces for 45N. The results are shown below.

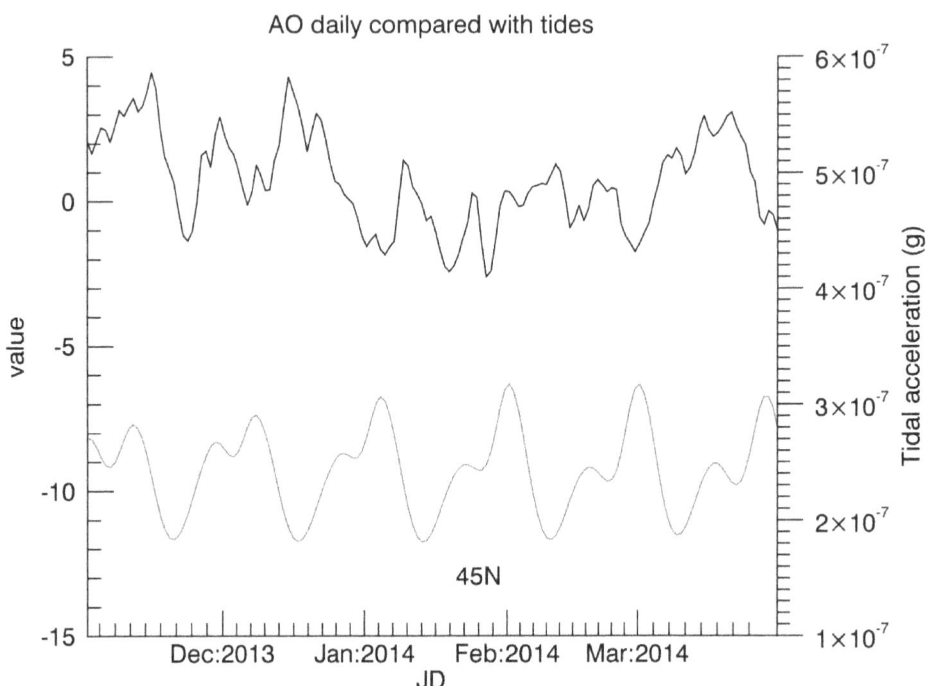

Winter 2013/14 AO compared to tidal tractional acceleration at 45°N
Again there is clear evidence that high latitude lunar tides modulated the Jet Stream. The severe storms in the UK caused coastal flooding because they coincided with high spring tides. Now I suspect that probably those high spring tides may have also have been a major cause of these very storms by also perturbing the Jet Stream!

*1 UNDERSTANDING TIDES

Posted on February 14, 2014 by Clive Best

There has been a long animated discussion about tides at Wattsupwiththat which highlighted a confusion about both the causes of tides and their strength. Several people are adamant that tides are a universal phenomena experienced by any object near a large gravitational source. They argue that tides are caused by the gradient of the 1/r^2 field.

While an extended object falling into a star or black hole will experience a transient tidal force, it is only bodies in orbit around each other that experience long term tidal forces acting on the surface. The earth is in orbit about the earth-moon barycenter. It is not in an inertial frame. It is in an accelerating frame of reference, similar to the way that the rotation of the earth about its axis causes a reduction in g at the equator.

So what is the real cause of tides on earth and why is the lunar tide larger than the solar tide ? Here is my derivation for the formulae for tides.

For 2 bodies in orbit the "centrifugal force" must balance the gravitational force. The centrifugal force is constant within a solid body in the same way that it is for a plate spinning on a stick.

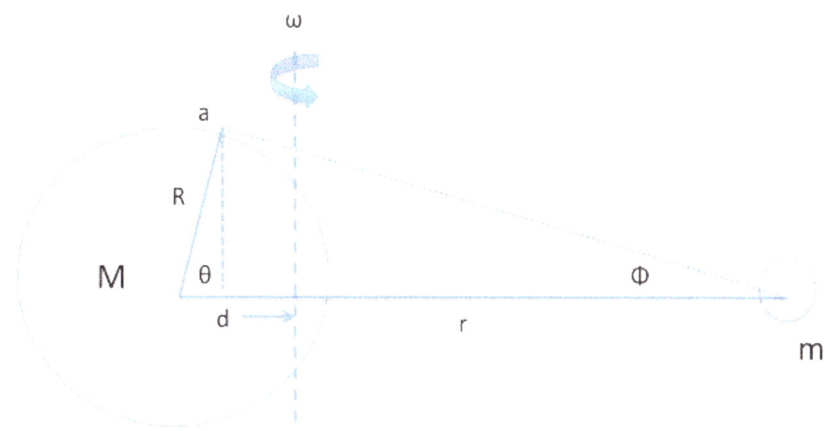

Fig 1

$$\frac{GMm}{r^2} = M\omega^2 d$$

Therefore the centrifugal acceleration on body M is $\omega^2 d = \frac{Gm}{r^2}$

Now consider the net force per unit mass acting on point a). Assuming that $\phi = 0$ we get

$$\frac{Gm}{(r - R\cos\theta)^2} - \frac{Gm}{r^2}$$
$$= \frac{Gm}{r^2}\left(\left(1 - \frac{R}{r\cos\theta}\right)^{-2} - 1\right)$$

assuming that r>>R we can do a binomial expansion to get

$$= \frac{Gm}{r^2}\left(1 + \frac{2R}{r}\cos\theta - 1\right)$$
$$= \frac{2GmR\cos\theta}{r^3}$$

This derives the approximate formula for the tidal force. There are two bulges centered on $\theta = 0 \,(and)\, \theta = \pi$

Now we can do the full calculation where the angle ϕ is no longer zero and thereby identify how the tidal force acquires a vertical component.

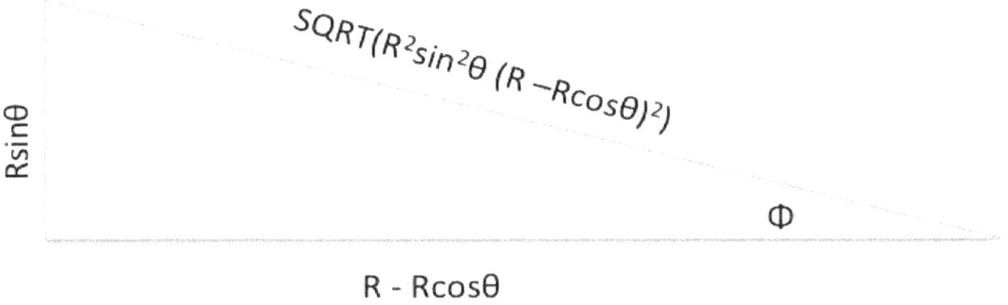

Calculation of the angle phi. Distance a-m is the hypotomuse
The distance a-m is by Pythagorus

$$\sqrt{R^2\sin^2\theta + (r - R\cos\theta)^2}$$

$$= \sqrt{R^2 + r^2 - 2rR\cos\theta}$$

Gravity acting on point a) is therefore $= \dfrac{Gm}{R^2 + r^2 - 2rR\cos\theta}$

Net tidal force now has 2 components

$$Fx = Gm\left(\frac{\cos\phi}{R^2 + r^2 - 2rR\cos\theta} - \frac{1}{r^2}\right)$$

$$Fy = \frac{-Gm\sin\phi}{R^2 + r^2 - 2rR\cos\theta}$$

where

$$\cos\phi = \frac{r - R\cos\theta}{\sqrt{R^2 + r^2 - 2rR\cos\theta}}$$

and

$$\sin\phi = \frac{R\sin\theta}{\sqrt{R^2 + r^2 - 2rR\cos\theta}}$$

Now let's compare the two solutions by calculating the effective tidal acceleration. Figure 3 shows the approximate formula in red and the two components of the exact result in blue.

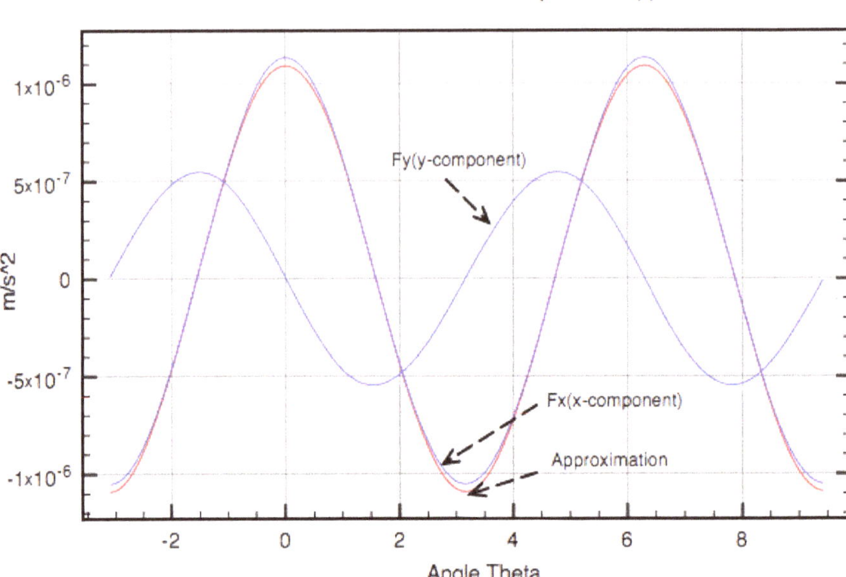

Fig 3: Comparison of the exact solution for tides with the approximation. There is now a significant vertical (y) component to the tidal force.

On earth the gravitational acceleration 'g' = 9.8 m/s^2 This can be compared with the above "tidal" accelerations of $\sim$ 10^-6 m/s^2. So the moon's tidal force is 10 million times less than the earth's gravitational force at the surface. This is not going to do any direct heavy lifting of the oceans! Instead it is the tractional component of the tidal force parallel to the surface which moves vast quantities of ocean. Now with the addition of the vertical component Fy the vector diagrams of tidal forces looks more like this:

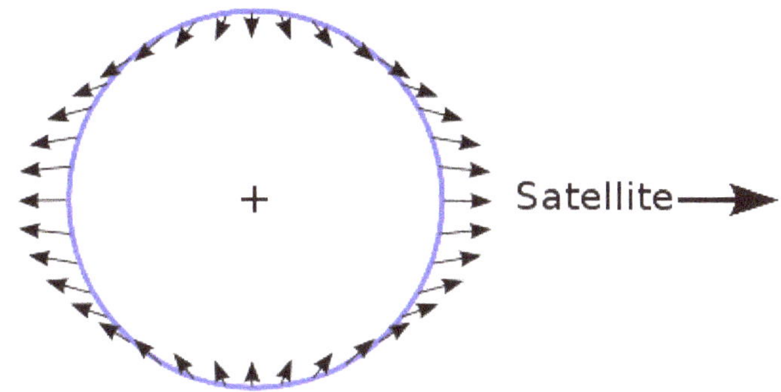

Fig 4: Vector diagram showing resultant tidal force (fx,Fy)

Note that the largest tractional forces are at larger theta angles. This drag of water currents throughout the depth of the ocean results in both tidal bulges. Figure 5 shows the tractional north-south force parallel to the earth's surface which is unaffected by the earth's gravity and therefore moves water from outside the bulge towards the centre.

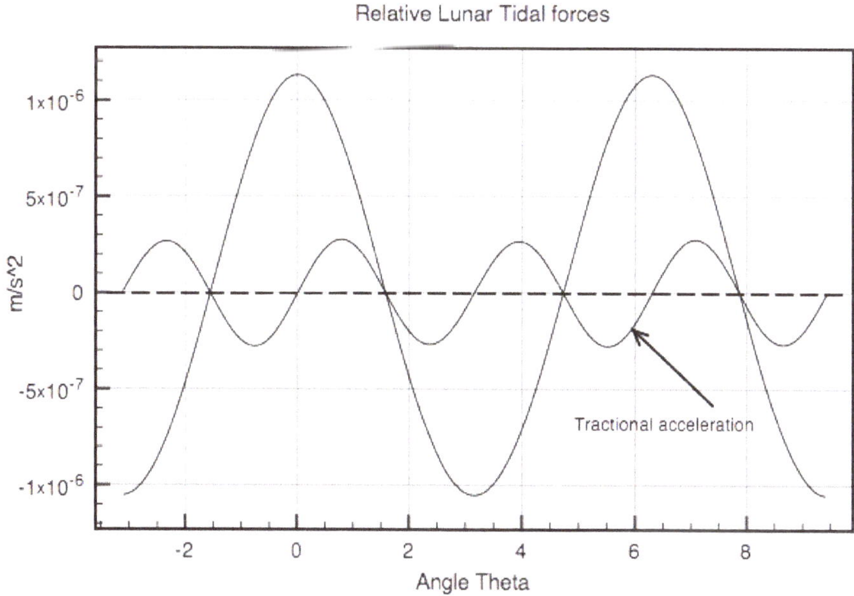

Fig 5: The tractional force moving vast quantities of water in the oceans to cause the tides.

The position and strength of these tractional forces is constantly changing during the lunar month, during the 18.6 year precession cycle and during longer time scale astronomical cycles. So the way I like to understand tides is that both the moon and the sun exert a horizontal drag force on the oceans and atmosphere. Twice a month we get spring tides when the sun and moon line up at new moon and the full moon, whose strength depends on the coincidence with both orbital perigees. Long term astronomical variations must have an effect on climate as orbital parameters slowly change increasing or decreasing ocean mixing and atmospheric dynamics.

Postscript

There is a <u>new argument about </u>whether centrifugal forces play any role at all in tides. In some sense both sides in this argument are correct. You **don't need** to use the centrifugal force to derive the formula for tides. This is because there is a perfect balance between the centrifugal force and the gravitational force at the center of the earth when in orbit around the earth-moon barycenter. This balance also determines the strength of tides on earth. When in doubt see what Feynman says.

What do we mean by "balanced"? What balances? If the moon pulls the whole earth toward it, why doesn't the earth fall right "up" to the moon? Because the earth does the same trick as the moon, it goes in a circle around a point which is inside the earth but not at its center. The moon does not just go around the earth, the earth and the moon both go around a central position, each falling toward this common position. This motion around the common center is what balances the fall of each. So the earth is not going in a straight line either; it travels in a circle. The water on the far side is "unbalanced" because the moon's attraction there is weaker than it is at the center of the earth, where it just balances the "centrifugal force." The result of this imbalance is that the water rises up, away from the center of the earth. On the near side, the attraction from the moon is stronger, and the imbalance is in the opposite direction in space, but again away from the center of the earth. The net result is that we get two tidal bulges.

A body in free fall into the sun experiences ever increasing tidal forces until it is torn apart. A body in orbit eperiences varying tidal forces depending on the eccentricity of the orbit. So on a purely logical basis Willis and Greg are correct because centrifugal forces don't enter into the formula for tides. However in order to calculate the variations of tides on earth you need to include orbital dynamics because they change the earth-moon distance.

HOW THE MOON AFFECTS THE WEATHER

Posted on August 4, 2014 by Clive Best

I aim to demonstrate in this series of posts that ever changing gravitational tides influence the flow of the polar Jet Stream thereby changing weather patterns at high latitudes. Such effects should be included in global circulation models to improve medium range weather forecasting.

Previously I described a proposal from Roberto Madrigali that tides acting on the Jet Stream affect high latitude weather (North and South). Robert Currie and others have reported long term coincidences of drought with Lunar Cycles (1). H. Yndestad reports lunar cycles in Arctic climates (2) and Li & Zong have reported lunar induced variations in global wind speed (3). Over 3000 years of folklore also links the moon to extreme weather on earth. Is all this just nonsense, or could atmospheric tides really be responsible for much of our weather in Europe and North America?

I decided to look into this in more detail and have spent the last few days calculating the horizontal tidal forces acting on the earth. To do this I used the JPL ephemeris to calculate the net tidal vector of the moon and the sun acting on the earth, and used the formulae derived previously to determine the horizontal tractional force for a given angular separation from the central net vector. In a north south direction this angular separation is the same as latitude. It is these tractional forces that cause the ocean currents that generate the two familiar tidal bulges. Although the forces are about 10 million times smaller than gravity they act perpendicular to gravity and cover vast regions of the earth. They also generate measurable winds in the upper atmosphere especially near the poles. The largest tractional forces occur at the extremes of latitude and can vary dramatically from month to month and year to year as the relative positions of the earth moon and sun change. The rotation of the earth then causes the familiar ~twice daily high tides. Their effect on the atmosphere is yet more complex also generating a small torque through the Coriolis effect.

The hypothesis presented here is that maximum tides induce meanders in the Jet Stream and mixing of warm and cold air masses which then trigger storm systems. I estimate that the horizontal force acting on a

1000km long stretch of the Jet Stream to be roughly half a billion newtons or the equivalent of 10,000 metric tonnes weight. My calculations for the year 2013/14 are shown below.

The animation shows a calculation of the horizontal tidal forces acting on the oceans and atmosphere as the moon and earth orbit both each other and the sun from 1 Oct 2013 until 30 September 2014. The daily variations are shown for a fixed longitude -30 deg. and show the maximum of either the lunar facing or the opposite tide. That is why the central bulge stays above the equator. Note that a series of severe storms hit the UK on Dec 5-6, Dec 23-24, Dec 26-27, Dec 30-31,Jan 3-6, Feb 4-5, Feb 12-14. This winter was a period of especially strong tides and this summer will see 3 super moons. The animation shows that the strongest tidal forces must affect the polar Jet Stream zone. Rapid changes in these tidal forces generate differential torques acting on the Jet Stream as the earth rotates by coriolis effects. Did these torques then trigger the destructive UK storms this winter?

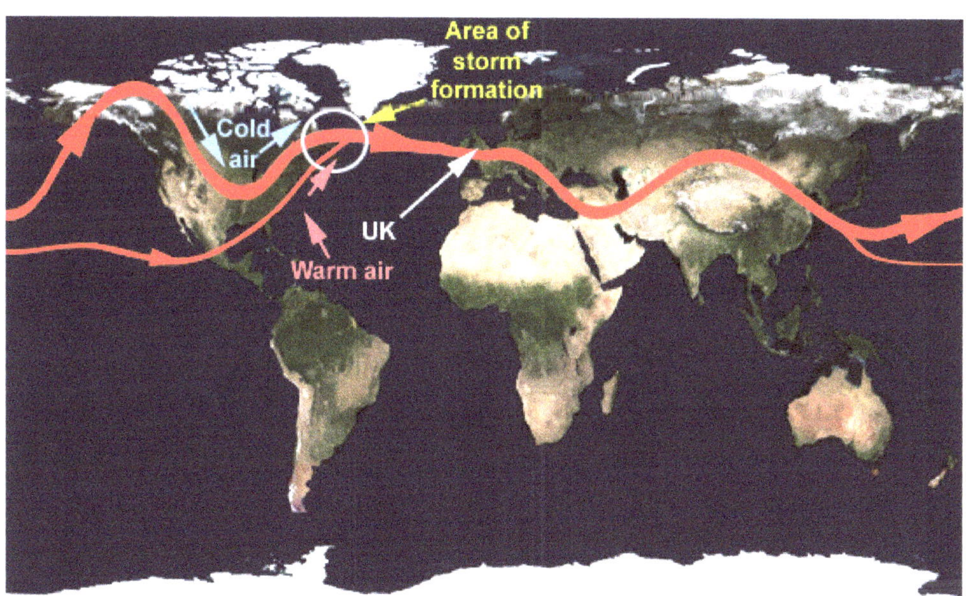

Rough position of Jet Stream during UK winter storms (Skeptical Science)

Meanders in the Jet Stream caused the extreme cold weather across North east America and also placed the UK directly in the firing line for Atlantic storms. Warm air sucked up from the Gulf created unstable conditions for storms to develop. The trigger for these storms seems likely to be rapid variations in atmospheric tides at the critical latitude. Judge for yourself.

Now we look more into the effects of the 18.6 year cycle, which is reported as being responsible for changes in rainfall across China and North America. In the following animation I just follow the lunar facing tide to show how strongly asymmetric the tides can get.

June 2006 saw a major lunar standstill. This is when the moon's orbit reached its maximum declination of 28.5 deg. The tidal bulge moves from a latitude of -28.5 deg to + 28.5 deg in about 14 days. This animation shows the tractional tidal force field centered on a longitude of -30 deg. Only the lunar facing tide is shown. In reality there are 2 high tides every day as the earth rotates through the lunar facing tide and its mirror on the earth's opposite side. Do such large changes in tidal forces tweak the Jet Stream mixing polar air with warm air thereby affecting weather systems ?

Ensemble model based forecasts are accurate over short terms. Would these be improved if tidal forces on the atmosphere were included? The evidence is that the answer is quite probably yes. Shown below is the 2 week prediction for London weather from today (August 4) by the Global Forecast System Ensemble of models prepared by Roberto Madrigali. A period of instability is expected exactly coincident with the largest "super-moon" tide this summer. Lets see what happens over the next 2 weeks.

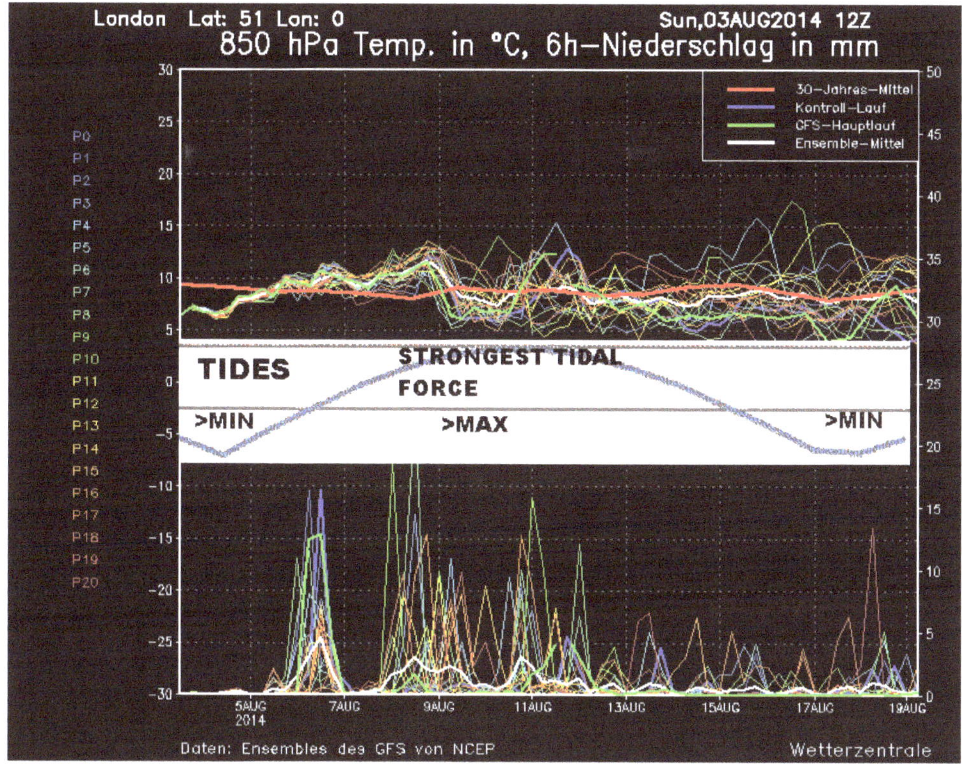

GFS Ensemble predictions for London for 4 August (the day I wrote this post). Top curves are temperature, bottom curves are precipitation. The maximum tidal forces are shown in the centre. The period of instability is synchronous with the extreme tidal maximum August 10th the 3rd super-moon of 2014 !

We often hear the analogy that because our weather is chaotic, storms can be generated just by the flapping of butterfly's wings. Well there is a prime candidate for that butterfly effect – the ever changing tides acting on the northern and southern Jet Streams! Perhaps its time now to take the moon more seriously !

1) Robert Currie, Periodic (18.6-YEAR) and cyclic (ll-YEAR) induced drought and flood in Western North America, JOURNAL OF GEOPHYSICAL RESEARCH, VOL. 89, NO. D5, PAGES 7215-7230, AUGUST 20, 1984

2) H. Yndestad, The influence of the lunar nodal cycle on Arctic climate, ICES Journal of Marine Science, Vol 63,3 P 401-420.

3) GuoQing Li, HaiFeng Zong, 27.3-day and 13.6-day atmospheric tide, Science in China Series D: Earth Sciences September 2007, Volume 50, Issue 9, pp 1380-1395

THE UK STORM OF DEC 5-6 2013

Posted on August 14, 2014 by Clive Best

This post will present evidence that strong tides were a primary cause of the December 5/6 storm that surged down the North Sea last winter. The first observation to be noted is the remarkable coincidence that all of the UK December storms coincided with maxima in tidal forces, as shown below.

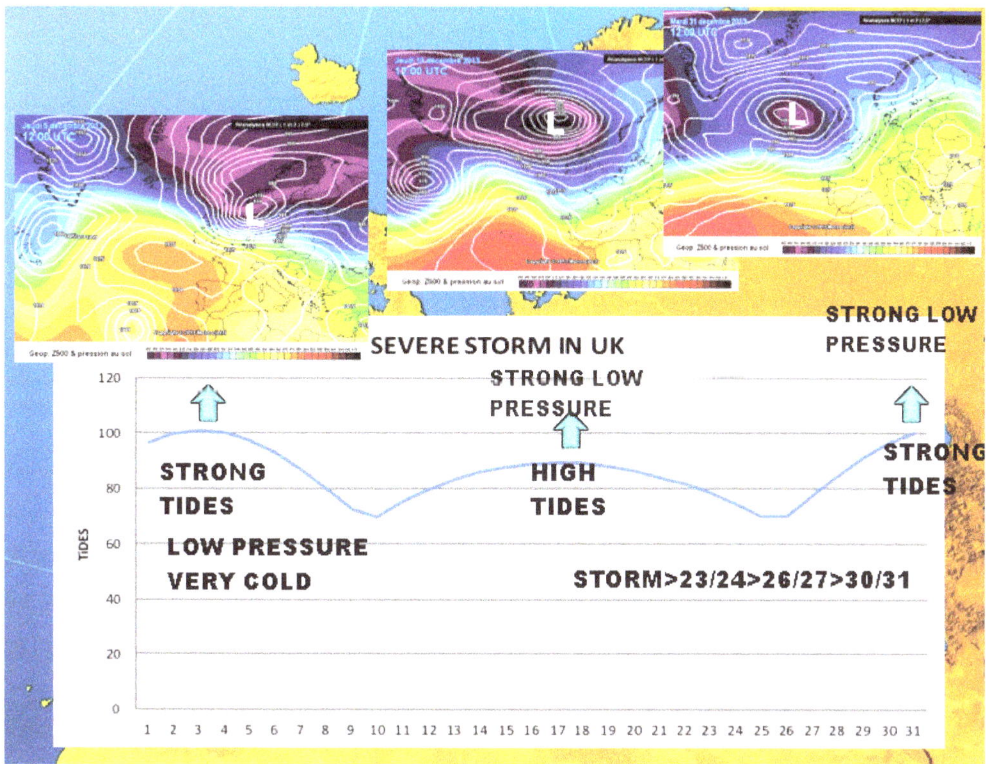

The December 2013 storms. This slide was prepared by Roberto Madrigali and shows how each successive storm coincided with maximum tidal forces. The strongest tide of all coincided with the December 5-6 storm.

So now let's look in detail at the first of these – 5/6 December storm. This first December storm also had the strongest tides of the year. The Met office writes the following description:

The first storm of 5 December brought very strong winds to Scotland and northern England, and a major storm surge affecting North Sea coasts. A week of quieter weather then followed, but from mid-December there was a succession of further major winter storms which continued into early January.

On the 3rd December a low depression system had already just passed north of the UK and appeared to be weakening. However for some reason it stalled and then strengthened on the 4th and 5th December while it descended south along the east coast of the UK. The associated storm surge caused extensive coastal flooding. This storm was very similar to the devastating 1953 storm which killed 300 people in the UK and over a thousand in the Netherlands. This experience led to the strengthening of coastal defenses and the eventual construction of the Thames barrage. This 1953 storm also coincided with a high spring tide and extensive storm surge.

Next we look at the evidence that it was these same strong tides that actually **caused** the storms. This evidence is based on the weather plots below shown below which track both the development of the storm and changes in the Jet Stream over the 3 day period beginning on the 4th December. All these charts are taken from meteociel.fr(2). These charts have been overlaid with arrows resulting from my calculations of the tractional vector tidal forces at the times shown. For comparison a deep red arrows correspond to a tidal acceleration of about $0.3*10^{-6}$ g.

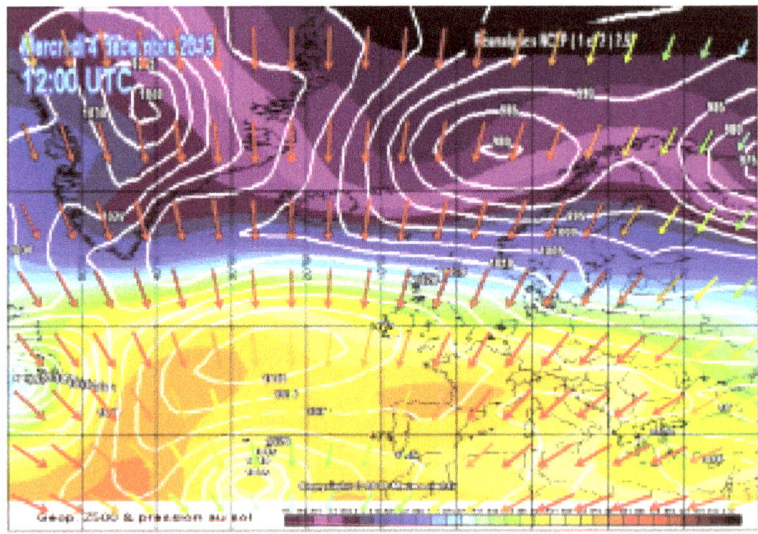

By midday on 4th December a depression had just passed over the UK and stalled to the North East of Scotland. The Jet Stream lay further south looping over the UK. The tides were increasing rapidly and strong tractional tidal forces were concentrated over northern polar latitudes tending to drag air south. These tidal forces are always changing as the earth rotates but during this period the moon's position was over the southern hemisphere causing asymmetric tides over the UK with one major tide effecting polar air masses every 24 hours. The net effect was to drag air down in a South-Easterly direction.

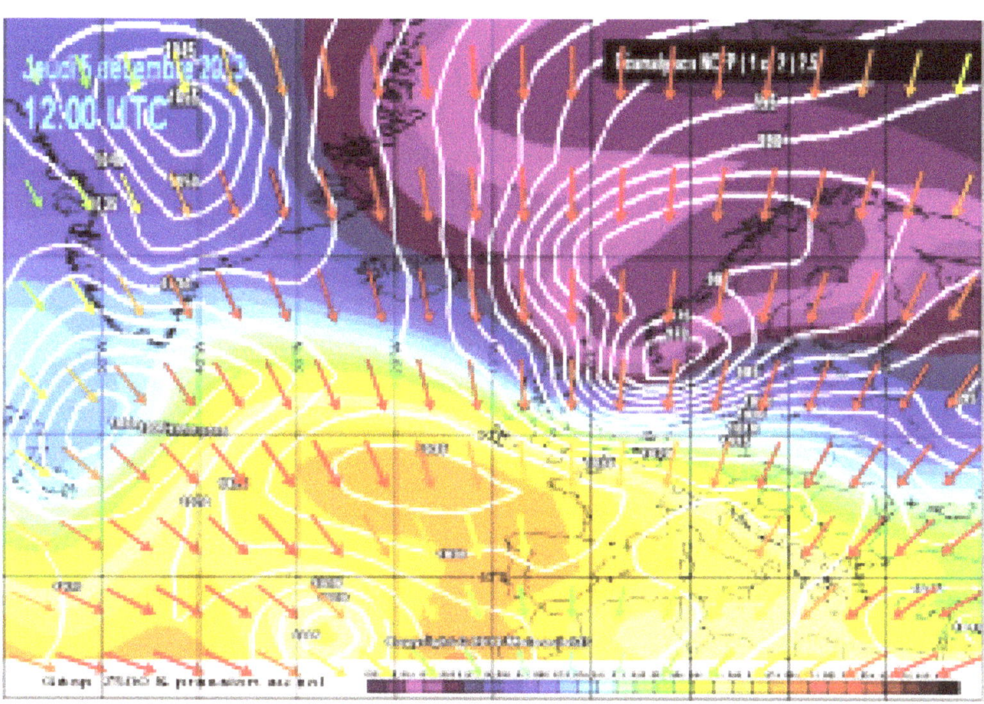

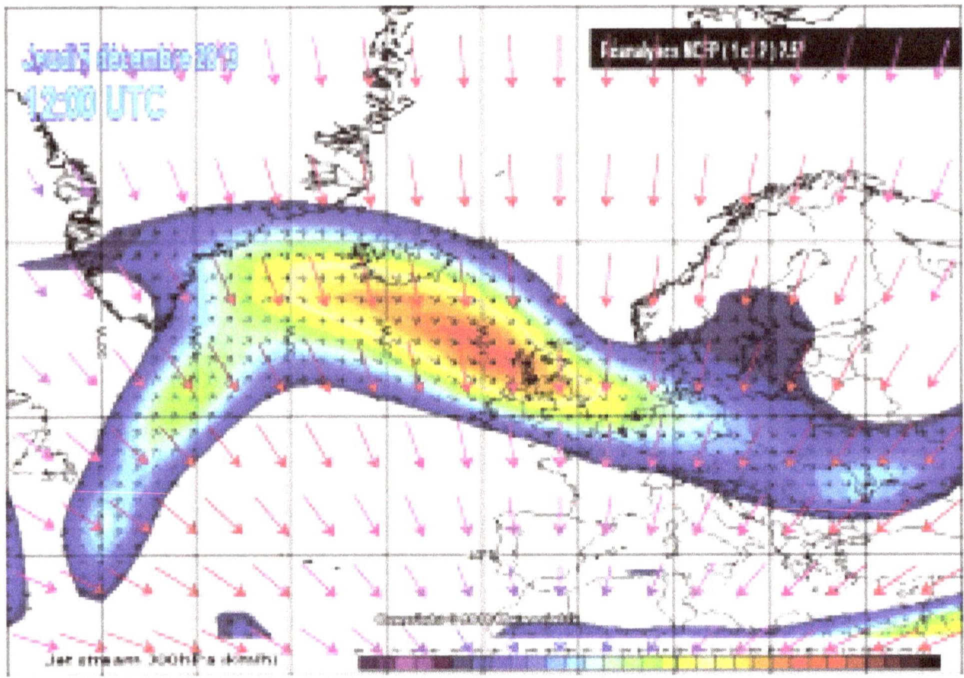

One day later on the 5th December the depression had now deepened and turned downwards towards Scotland bringing very strong winds to the north east coast. Tides still remained very high but now the Jet stream shows a southerly kink pulling to the east of the UK with very strong velocities. The arrows show the focussing effect of the tidal forces acting directly on the Jet Stream. The storm is now well underway and moving down the North Sea.

The Jet Stream remained strong for the next 24 hours and lay further south than is normal during the winter period. At the same time very cold polar air was drawn down over the east coast of the US.

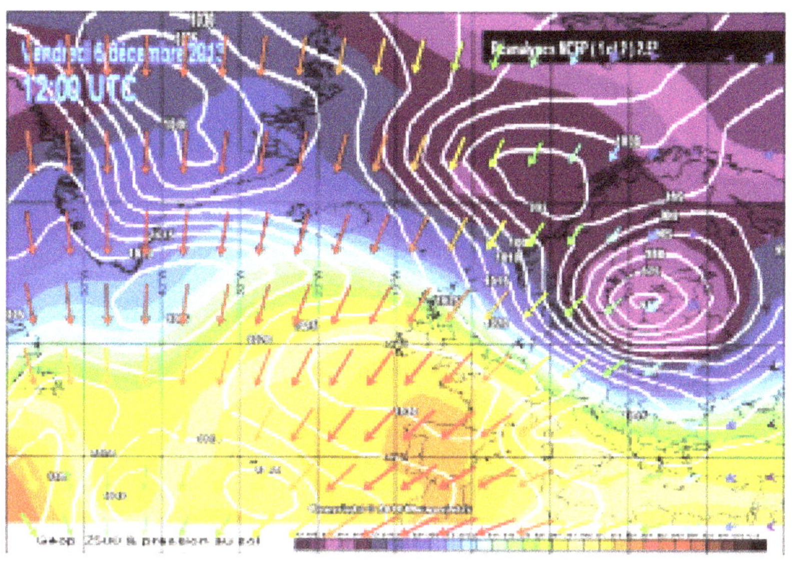

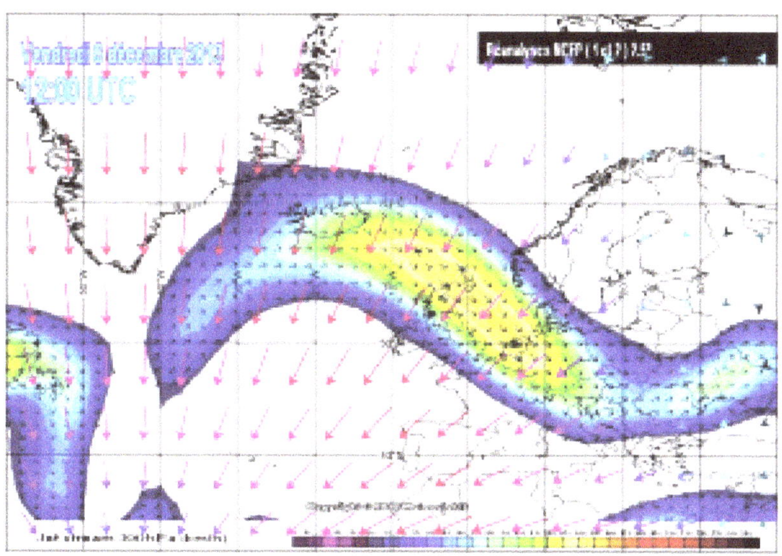

By 6th December there was a strong easterly flow of the Jet Stream driving the storm down the North Sea. This was then exacerbated by high maritime tides in the North Sea to create a storm surge similar to that in 1953. However this time there was far better warning, flood protection and preparation, but still hundreds were evacuated from their homes. By midday on the 6th December the storm center had moved off further to the east of the UK still leaving strong north easterly winds.

The BBC reported the effects of the this first storm of the winter as follows:

Tidal surge hits east UK coastal towns after storm

The tidal surge which hit the east coast of Britain has been described as the "most serious" for 60 years.

Thousands were forced to abandon their homes as tides in parts of the North Sea reached higher levels than the devastating floods of 1953.

Flood waters have receded in many areas but authorities are warning that high tides later on Friday could cause further damage.

Maxima in spring tides only last a few days as the moon rapidly moves out of phase with the sun during its 28 day orbit. Possible effects on weather at high latitudes are stronger in winter because a) there is often a strong asymmetry between the two tidal bulges and b) there are far less thermal tides in polar regions due low to zero solar radiation.

Horizontal tidal forces may appear to be weak because they are about 2 million times less than the earth's gravitational force. However there is no opposing force parallel to the earth's surface. It is these tractional forces that generate the tidal bulges in the oceans and coastal tides. They act over vast areas and their effects are strongest at high latitudes.

In summary the first major storm of lhen ast winter on 5-6th December corresponded to the largest spring tides of the year. These tidal forces were strongest north of the Jet Stream and appear to have drawn down a passing depression and in the process strengthened it into a major storm hitting the east coast of the UK.

Future posts we will look at the other UK storms during the winter of 2013/14 and investigate whether they too show any causal connection with changing atmospheric tides.

Notes

1. Roberto Madrigali was one of the first to propose a connection between lunar tides and weather.

2. All jet stream images and weather maps are produced curtesy of meteociel.fr

3. I am not a meteorologist !

Figure 10.45. Himalaya.

Figure 10.46. Himalaya, climbing on Tengi–Rau–Tau, the passage of an avalanche.

Figure 10.47. East Greenland, volcanic area of Jamson Land.

Figure 10.48. Greenland, geothermal.

Figure 10.49. East Greenland, glacial fjord.

Figure 10.50. East Greenland.

Figure 10.51. Gran Sasso tunnel.

Figure 10.52. Gran Sasso at sunset.

Figure 10.53. Gran Sasso, towards the high peak.

Figure 10.54. Gran Sasso, spring 2013.

Figure 10.55. Gran Sasso, spring 2013.